PRAISE FOR
WORD SHIFT

"Joy Kirr's book, *Word Shift*, is an important book for all educators because it draws attention to both the potential harm and the benefits of labels, especially when we apply them to students. Joy reminds us that unleashing true potential begins by removing the labels that hold our children hostage."

—**Jimmy Casas**, educator, author, speaker, leadership coach

"*Word Shift* was a joy to read. It helped me reflect on the words and phrases commonly used in our field, along with rationale as to why some of them are so problematic. Additionally, it provided sentence starters and suggestions for topics that we should be talking about. I highly recommend this book, and can't wait to participate in the ensuing conversations that it will, no doubt, spark within our community."

—**Sarah Thomas, PhD**, founder, EduMatch

"I never realized how much the words I use affected what I thought or became. In *Word Shift*, Joy Kirr personalizes words in a dictionary form by listing words to reflect upon before using, with reasons why and alternatives to consider. Using more precise words that give a clearer message made me see why I'm not a 'blogger,' I'm an 'inquirer.' I don't give 'feedback,' I provide 'feedforward' for more positive support. To take the words a step further, Kirr shares labels and adjectives that best describe students and peers. She lists topics, phrases, and questions to consider discussing throughout the school year. *Word Shift* is just what every educator and parent needs on their bookshelves to pull out when wondering what and how to say something with their children."

—**Barbara Bray**, creative learning strategist, author

"What you say to a student can stick with them for a lifetime. In *Word Shift*, Kirr provides a comprehensive list of words to think about or rethink in their use in education, not to pursue getting every person to think the same way, but to get every person that works with children to think about how we can elevate our students to their fullest potential. I appreciate Kirr's focus on being intentional in a positive manner with how we talk to our students, our colleagues, and ourselves, to bring out the best in those that surround us."

—**George Couros,** author of *The Innovator's Mindset*

"Words have incredible power! *Word Shift* captures the importance of using positive language when expressing opinions and talking with others. Inspired by the voices of her students, this book explores the impact educators have while reflecting on their mindset, their beliefs, and their educational convictions. Positivity and optimism create lasting change; it is up to educators to embrace their why and lead the revolution. Joy's vision and heart flow on every page of this book, which is a must-read for all educators."

—**Roman Nowak**, high school English language arts teacher

"This book is a quick read that can be applied immediately to one's practice. It provides an opportunity to start a conversation as a staff about common language that can be used to develop a positive school culture."

—**Martin Ruthaivilavan**, international educator

"Our words matter and last long after they leave our lips. Once it's been said, you cannot unsay it.

"Joy has chosen words that are commonly used in the education environment and provided a thought-provoking perspective on why they have no place here. As I read each word, its common usage, then Joy's perspective, I find I am reflecting on and analyzing my own word usage.

"A word or phrase may have a particular meaning to one person, but it can mean something completely different, even be offensive, in a different culture or circumstance. *Word Shift* encourages you to think about perspective, to show respect, and to use words to build relationships—not for compliance and power.

"Many references and links have been provided in *Word Shift* to give a broader perspective. Not only does *Word Shift* shift your thinking about which words we use the book also offers a section for positive alternatives. *Word Shift* aims to show you how to use words with a positive approach, and Joy delivers this beautifully. Joy is an inspiration, and I'm grateful for her words and their positive impact on me."

—**Catherine Williams**, K–6 teacher

WORD SHIFT

A Different Kind of Dictionary for
Educators to *Nullify Negativity* and
PROMOTE POSITIVITY
in Schools!

JOY KIRR

WORD SHIFT

© 2019 by Joy Kirr

This book is available at special discounts when purchased in quantity for use as premiums, promotions, fundraisers, or for educational use. For inquiries and details, contact the publisher at books@daveburgessconsulting.com.

Published by Dave Burgess Consulting, Inc.
San Diego, CA
http://daveburgessconsulting.com

Cover Design by Genesis Kohler
Editing and Interior Design by My Writers' Connection

Library of Congress Control Number: 2019944126
Paperback ISBN: 978-1-949595-56-7
Ebook ISBN: 978-1-949595-57-4

First Printing: August 2019

CONTENTS

FOREWORD

You never know what kind of teachers you might get. You might get a "sugar" or "marshmallow" teacher, which means a nice teacher who doesn't yell. But there's always the "evil" teacher. That doesn't mean they're a witch with potions—it just means they're a little mean and might yell. Like most students, I have faced both.

In my elementary school, we had an amazing music teacher. You would walk into her classroom and see all the instruments that filled the room. She had a big piano that we would gather around and sing. She put her soul into our shows. In first grade, for the "Pirate Christmas" show, all of us little six-year-olds were dressed up as miniature elves, and the big fifth graders were the pirates. In second grade, the show was "Squirm," and groups of about twenty were different insects or gross things like worms or bats. In third grade, it was "The World." Every planet had a costume and a little solo to talk about their planet. And in fourth grade, the show was "Summer Camp." We had a party to make everyone a tie-dyed shirt, and we even had two bears.

This teacher taught us a song with all the presidents and hand motions to remember each one. Every day was a new adventure. We never knew what she would teach us next! She taught us many songs that helped with history. We learned more history in music class than in social studies. This teacher was definitely a "sugar" teacher and had a kind heart and taught us to be nice to everyone.

—Emma, eighth grader

Throughout the 2017–2018 school year, Joy and I asked our co-taught ELA seventh graders for feedback. On the last day of school, we asked the students summative questions: "What did you enjoy about our class?" and "Where could we, as teachers, improve?" Emma responded she was glad we didn't yell at them or say things like, "I'll chop off your knee caps," or "I'll light you on fire." Her words inspired Joy to stop simply collecting language teachers use, and start writing about it.

In my teaching career, I too have heard teachers use harmful language toward students, such as calling them stupid, idiots, or telling some they're a cool kid, but others are not. Just as we want students to reflect and grow, teachers need to reflect and grow. Teachers need to hear from their students. Without feedback from others and time to reflect, our growth is limited to our own perspectives. The way you think about your students influences how you treat them. I believe my students are courageous, curious learners who are deserving of empathy, even during their worst day.

—*Yvette Rehberger, special education teacher*

WHY A DICTIONARY?

why—*adv.* For what purpose, reason, or cause; with what intention, justification, or motive

[*The American Heritage Dictionary*, fourth edition, Houghton Mifflin Harcourt (2009)]

There is no getting around the truth: Education is a difficult profession. Yes, there are days when all the effort seems more than worth it. Those rewarding moments keep us coming back for more. Then there are days (lots of them) when our exhaustion levels peak, when our home life invades our school life, and we're at an energy level of zero before we even see our first class. It's those stressful moments that add up and take their toll.

Although I have not formally studied stress, I have felt its effects. If you work in education, I'm sure you've felt it too. Stress can affect our thoughts, feelings, health (mental and physical), and behavior. Stress can keep us from sleeping, affect our appetite (causing us to eat too much or to skip meals), and even cause some people to drink in excess.

Educators at every level are actively seeking ways to deal with the stress that comes with being a teacher. We download mindfulness apps, journal, join meditation classes, and attend retreats—all in the hope of finding relief.

THE STRESS WE FEEL IS REAL.

I'm aware that there are "good" stressors (challenges that help us grow) and "bad" stressors (those that can harm us). Sadly, the kind of stress we feel as educators tends to be more harmful than helpful, and it can even be contagious. It is passed like a virus when we let some of the stress-induced, nasty, or hurtful things we're thinking slip through our lips. It happens. I've done it. Those words—sometimes used in the classroom but more often whispered in the workroom or shouted in the staff parking lot after a particularly tough day—can infect the culture of the entire school.

I've met and have worked with many students, educators, and school administrators throughout my lifetime. I have heard those working in schools say some of the most kind, perfect-for-the-situation words. And I've heard some say the vilest things—even about those we instruct. I thought about listing the words I've overheard in an appendix to this book but thought better of it; I wouldn't want young eyes to catch sight of them. And, frankly, I want to forget I ever heard them. My bet is, if you can think it, it's been said.

After reading *Choice Words* by Peter Johnston in 2014, I felt inspired to watch what I say and write. I've since tried to use precise words that accurately portray the message I want to convey in my blogs, on social media, and in face-to-face conversations. It's an endeavor that comes with a few challenges because words have nuanced meanings, and those meanings may change over time.

Remember when "sick" meant someone had the flu? I remember "bombing" tests. Now if it's "the bomb," it's a good thing! Country star Tim McGraw sang about this shift in meaning in his song "Back When." I couldn't help but think of that shift when I told someone I had gone shopping and picked the "*baddest* sweet potato the store had"— and I actually meant the "best"! Language and messages change at a rapid pace, due in part to the fact that we have myriad ways to instantly communicate with people globally. This instantaneous communication makes words spread—and morph—like wildfire. Give this book a year, and some of these phrases will change once again.

Word usage changes based on who we are, who we're with, and how we're feeling. You've probably known that person who uses foul language with you, and then not around children. Or that same person might use different words with their spouse and again change them depending on what friends are near. Often, it's my emotions and what's happened in my life recently that dictate the words that come out of my own mouth.

The more I think about words and their impact, the more firmly I believe that we must be precise and intentional with the way we express our thoughts. That may mean we need to reconsider some words—particularly words that may have different meanings than they did only a few years (or weeks) ago. I've also noticed that when we, as educators, administrators, and parents, choose the right words, we can elicit more thinking and action in our students and show more care.

We can start by thinking about the labels that are so prevalently used in the school system. Labels—whether we think them or say them aloud—influence the way we feel about people. They limit our students, confining them to the borders of the label, and for that reason alone, I want to stop labeling students, even in my mind. The truth is, I will most likely slip up from time to time, but my daily goal is to remember to ask, "Why is this person acting this way?" rather than attaching a derogatory label to a child or coworker. Changing labels is where I've started this book, because using labels is something I've noticed myself doing on a regular basis. Throughout *Word Shift*, you'll find various labels that I've heard used or have used myself, and at the end of this "dictionary" I've included a list of words we could be using instead to help empower our students and colleagues.

I know that the words I use will ultimately affect what I think and who I become, as I've experienced how language affects my own thinking. For instance, when I hear a teacher using a label to define certain students, I instinctively attach that label to the students. I've applied fresh labels to students, even after they've been in my class for months, when I heard another teacher say, "Oh, Joy. You have some mean girls in that class." What? Who? Suddenly I saw those girls differently. I noticed the eye rolls, the scoffs, the way they talked with one another in class. Should I have noticed those things before? Perhaps. What hurt, however, was that, for the rest of the school year, I saw the "mean girl" label on those students *every day*. I became aware of every tiny action that reinforced my new perception of them as mean girls.

3

To remove that label, I needed to alter my perspective. I needed to look for the good. I needed to remember that maybe, in a classroom situation, one or more of these girls had *acted* "mean." Furthermore, I needed to remember that when I saw one of these girls huddled with another, it was *not* necessarily proof that they were scheming or talking about another student. And I needed to remember that even a particular behavior in class did not necessarily indicate those girls were in any way mean on their own. Or at home. Or … consider the possibilities! Also consider that had I not heard that I had the "mean girls" in my class, I would have been able to see more of the positives of what they were doing in class and could have called them out on that behavior. Had I reinforced the goodness or kindness I saw in them, maybe they would have had a better chance of shedding the "mean girl" label and truly changing their behavior.

When I realized I had been putting labels on students and peers, I started noticing other words I was using and words that were uttered in my presence. I've been there. I've done that. I have labeled students, peers, and even family without really knowing the entire story. Without delving further by asking questions, I've judged without much reason. But I'm trying to grow.

I wrote this book for myself, first and foremost. You may not agree with it all. It may even stir up some uncomfortable conversations. In fact, I am determined to stay away from reviews online, because I'll bet some readers will be very particular in their word choice about what they get out of this book (if anything). The thoughts expressed in this book are simply my opinion. This work is not based on research; it grew out of my twenty-four-plus years of experience as an educator. Like other dictionaries, this book is not designed to be read straight through. It is meant to be used as a reference and as a guide to help us all find and use words that promote a more positive school culture.

Be careful how you are talking to yourself because you are listening.

~Lisa M. Hayes

I FOUND THIS POSTED AT A LOCAL HIGH SCHOOL, AND IT RINGS SO TRUE!

4

Our thoughts become our words, and our words become our actions. I'd like to work in a positive environment that nurtures life-long learners. You most likely would too, since you're still reading.

In *1984*, by George Orwell, "The Party" was working on the eleventh edition of the Newspeak dictionary. In that fictional world, fewer words are better, as there is less need for thought. Thought (according to members of "The Party") is dangerous. As I was in the midst of writing *Word Shift*, I read *1984* for the first time, and the thought (dangerous, I know) came to me that we should have more words so we can accurately depict what we wish to say. We need more precise words so we can have conversations in which our messages are conveyed more clearly and where more discussion—instead of more frustration—follows. You may notice that I frequently use the words "I believe" and "let's." I hope you get the sense that we're in this together. I'm not here to tell you what to do or not do.

My sincere hope is that we will all use words that will push us toward better outcomes—as individuals, schools, and as a society. We can perform our own action research in our schools. I would love for anyone who works with children to eliminate certain words from their vocabulary in the school setting. As a reading specialist and language arts teacher, I know the precise words are out there. Let's find them and use them.

Irony: One of the words in here is *don't*. Throughout these pages, some could say I'm saying "don't" to many words. I hope you won't feel that way. These are words that I myself still sometimes use. I'm human. I have strong emotions. I make mistakes. I do not want to put anyone down for using these words; I simply want us (yes, including me) to continually reflect on the language we are using with children and with our peers.

I'd love your feedback, advice, and suggestions on this book. Although I have almost a quarter century of experience as an educator, I have only one life story. Your perspective and experience will be different from my own. I invite you to connect with me via Twitter (@JoyKirr) or through comments on my blog (geniushour.blogspot. com) to share your thoughts and opinions. Feedback sometimes hurts, even if it's done with utmost respect, but I value it as a tool to develop further as an educator.

As you're reading **Word Shift**, annotate in the margins to contribute your own word choices, then share them with me using the hashtag #WordShift on your favorite social media platform. As you're listening in school, add to this dictionary and share the alternative word choices you've discovered with your peers! Let's keep talking, keep reflecting, and keep sharing.

A note about the photos—For one of our "questions of the day," I asked my seventh graders to write down what they wish teachers would stop saying. You'll see their insights throughout this book.

6

WORDS TO REFLECT UPON BEFORE USING, REASONS WHY, AND ALTERNATIVES TO CONSIDER

ACT YOUR AGE

If we stop and think about it, our students most likely are acting their age. Their decision-making isn't up to par with adults, as the frontal lobe takes quite a few years to develop. They probably don't know what it means to act their age, as they've never been this age before. Instead of telling a child to "act your age," let's try explaining our expectations for behavior. "Try to sit still for a moment," "Speak in a softer voice," or "Remember to be kind" could be easier for our students to understand and try to do. Children need specific instructions, then they need time to practice these skills.

ALL/ALWAYS/EVERY/NEVER/NONE (ABSOLUTES)

Absolutes "never" go over well. In my move toward shifting to more precise language, I am working on saying what I mean, not what I feel. I've noticed, for example, that after a lesson flops, I may *feel* as if I never want to try that lesson again. I know, though, that I can reflect on ways to improve the lesson, I will have different students next year, and I will have opportunities to try it again.

Absolutes break down when we look at them from different perspectives. Even on those days when it seems that *every* student is "acting out" or "disruptive," if I take a closer look, I can see the good. When I take a second look, I can notice that not "all" of my students are acting one way or the other. We have a wide variety, and it's good to notice this before we make a statement using an absolute.

ALLOW/LET/PERMIT

Instead of *permitting* or *allowing* students to do something, maybe we could "provide opportunities" or "encourage" students to, for

7

example, go to the washroom. Does it mean I'm a pushover if I don't act like a boss and "allow" students to use the washroom or "let" them use my pencil? No. I'm trying to treat students as humans.

Perhaps, rather than focusing on our rules, we could address student choices. Consider the choices we make during the day that we don't have to ask permission to do. Could we offer these same opportunities for students? If a student asks to do something, I'd like to reply with, "Why not?" so the student can think about the ramifications for that certain choice. If there are no negative consequences, I think these choices should be "allowed" without much thought from the teacher. We could then be guides for students as they consider such choices as going back to their locker for supplies or taking a break to get a drink of water.

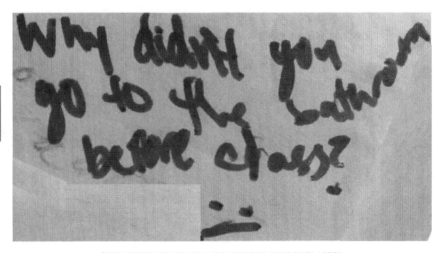

"WHY DIDN'T YOU GO TO THE BATHROOM BEFORE CLASS?"

ASSUME

Maybe you are already aware of what assuming can make out of "u" and "me." It's only natural. As humans, we make snap judgments. We judge based on appearance first, and those judgments are formed by our (known and hidden) biases. I propose we recognize these biases and the assumptions that come with them and ask ourselves more questions to clarify. Questions such as "What am I missing?" or "Is there more to the story than this?" will help us refocus if we're assuming something that might, in fact, be a misunderstanding. If you need more convincing that making assumptions is a bad habit, check out educator/administrator and author Jeff Zoul's blog titled "Stop Making Assumptions" (**bit.ly/WSassume**). If we must make assumptions, let's try to start with an open mind and make positive assumptions first.

BAD APPLES (AS A LABEL)

I had a parent tell me on open house night, "I think it's hard for my child to be in a class with 'bad apples.'" I have no memory of how I responded, only that I was shocked by her choice of words to describe some bad behaviors she'd heard about from her child. In schools, our learners range in age from three to twenty-one. The human brain is not fully developed until somewhere between twenty-two and twenty-five.

If you have the growth mindset like I do, you believe that all children can change their ways if they have enough guidance and the intrinsic motivation to do so. By calling children "bad apples" or saying, "The apple doesn't fall far from the tree," we are defining their future before they've had a chance to become who they will be.

I know some educators who believe that people cannot change and that people are innately "good" or "bad." If that's you, please reconsider that belief. You could be the person with the ability to guide students to change their behavior and their life. The words you use to describe them will make all the difference.

BEHAVIOR PROBLEM (AS A LABEL)

Whose problem is it? I will not label students as "behavior problems." Children may have trouble controlling their behavior, but *they* are not problems. Instead of labeling a student, consider describing that child's actions instead. Then try to figure out what caused the student to behave in that fashion. Use that insight to brainstorm ways to help that student behave in a different way.

Ask the students themselves what guides their behaviors, and what their goals are for themselves. Consider working with them to see why their behavior is causing other people problems.

BLAME

We have many reasons to be upset during the course of a school year. Sometimes it feels good to take time to figure out who is to blame for our circumstances. Consider turning the discussion to look for the good to share instead. Even in a frustrating situation, be intentional about showing gratitude for those who are doing things right, and share the goodness. Let's move from "blame" to "credit" or "compliment." Let's credit or compliment someone instead of focusing on what's wrong, and, in turn, lift the spirits of those around us. Help them build on their strengths. Then we'll take a look at that problem again and see how we or our peers can either begin to solve it or figure out a way to move on from it.

BLOGGER (AS A LABEL)

Why is this person blogging? Publicizing, sharing, self-promoting, connecting…? Try "publicist," "inquirer," or refer to that person as "one who contributes to conversations." Those who blog are "writers" and also "authors." How wonderful that our students, educators, and administrators can be *authors* who are sharing their vulnerability by publishing their thoughts and encouraging further conversations!

BOYS AND GIRLS (OR LADIES AND GENTLEMEN)

Many teachers have male and female students in their classrooms. Other classrooms are popping up all over (and they may have been there all along) with students who are transgender or identify as gender-fluid. Gender identity and sexual identity have evolved, and many of us are far behind in knowing how to speak to students without harming them mentally. Try using words that describe what students should be doing, such as "readers," "researchers," "historians," "scientists," "mathematicians," or even "scholars" or "students." This may also have a side effect of redirecting those that are off task. See the list of "Labels That Build up Students and Peers" at the end of this book.

BRAINIAC (AS A LABEL)

"Brainiac," to a student, may imply "nerd." Let's recognize the various talents and skills our students display, without labeling them into a corner. When learners who are labeled as brainiacs come across something difficult, they may feel like failures if they can't find the solution on their own. Let's give them the tools to overcome that feeling of failure and empower them to learn from their struggles and mistakes. Let's talk more about skills students are developing, such as perseverance and adaptability.

BUCK UP/DEAL WITH IT

"Deal with it" was my line during my high school years. I remember using a marker and writing it on all my class folders. Now, when I think of saying it, I remember learning about kids who cannot "deal with it."

Some of our students have gone through such trauma or life changes that they do not know how to "buck up" or "deal with it." Maybe they've already tried different tactics, and none have worked (so far). Maybe they've heard these phrases too many times, and we become just "one of those people" who cannot help them.

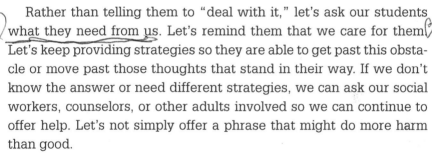

Rather than telling them to "deal with it," let's ask our students what they need from us. Let's remind them that we care for them. Let's keep providing strategies so they are able to get past this obstacle or move past those thoughts that stand in their way. If we don't know the answer or need different strategies, we can ask our social workers, counselors, or other adults involved so we can continue to offer help. Let's not simply offer a phrase that might do more harm than good.

BUT

"I love that you got the right answer, but you went about it the wrong way." That little word "but" negates any positive word that came before it. The only time "but" is effective is when it's used after something not so good, such as, "You went about this problem the wrong way, *but* you still got the right answer. Show me what you did here."

Substituting "however" for "but" doesn't make a positive difference; it's basically the same thing. Educator Abe Moore (@Arbay38) saw me tweet about this idea and was doubtful. He then tried to eliminate "but" during conferences with students and when providing feedback and decided conferring and feedback were stronger without it. What has worked as an alternative is the word "and." Read the blog post, **"Words to Use with Caution: 'But'"** for more ideas to ponder **(bit.ly/WSbutcaution).**

BUTTHEAD/GOOFBALL/ANY OTHER "SILLY" DEROGATORY NAME HERE (AS A LABEL)

I've called kids "goofballs." I used to call my niece and nephew "goofball" until they started repeating the word when they began speaking ("Oof bah!"). I've heard teachers call their students "buttheads" and have heard some students call their teachers "butthead" back! What type of culture does that promote? Even when said nicely, such as saying, "Only my favorite buttheads get to use that stapler," in a warm or sweet tone of voice, these phrases don't have a sweet sound to them. It could be that the student themselves, their peers, or other teachers think those labels are rude. (Can you blame them?) Yes, there are worse words; these words are kinder than some you'll hear floating around the school corridors. Even so, let's find some substitutes that actually are kind.

CAN'T

Many times, we use the word "can't" as a matter of skill, when sometimes it is only a matter of will. When we develop or change our mindset, it becomes clear that there are many things we actually *can* do but *choose* not to do for some reason. What obstacles are stopping us? What makes us say, "can't"? Time to dig deeper.

> **"Those who say it can't be done are usually interrupted by others doing it."**
>
> —*James Baldwin*

CHANGE

There are myriad books on how to lead change or transform schools. It's a tough sell because the truth is, the word "change" can scare peers and children. Even if change is much needed, a different word choice can be more effective in promoting it. If what you're looking to do is not massive, consider using words such as "shift," "pivot," "adjust," "tweak," or "update." These words seem more friendly and more feasible.

CHEAT

If you think your students are cheating, consider the tasks you're asking them to do. If they're cheating by looking up something online, maybe the questions you're asking aren't making them think. When my students look up something online, I see it as them using their resources. If they're using their resources to look up a word they don't know so they can answer a question, is that cheating? Wouldn't we do the same? If they're looking up a solution to a math problem, and we're asking them to show their work, maybe they're looking up the right answer to see where they need to end up or to see if they're correct. (This may actually help them figure out how to show their work.) If the answers to our questions can be found online, maybe we need to rethink our assignment or assessment, or maybe we need to let them use the resources to find these answers and create something new from them. If many students seem to be looking at another student's work, consider making it partner work or share your reasons WHY it should be done individually. I've also seen (Or . . . maybe it was me?) students saying they completed four laps around the course when they'd only done three. It's now time to figure out how to help them accomplish this feat so they don't feel as if they need to take this type of shortcut.

See also: "trick them"

CLASS CLOWN

I've seen teachers and parents alike label children as the class clown. Students will own this title. My husband was called the class clown as a boy. He grew up before there were labels like ADD and ADHD, before we had differentiated plans for helping students with different needs. He is now collecting retirement from Ford, where he served for twenty-eight years in the refrigeration and air conditioning field. He worked with his hands and, in the process, learned to slow down and focus on what was needed.

Some "class clowns" act out as a way to cover their own insecurities regarding academics. Others are just happy people who like to make those around them laugh. Instead of sticking this label on students, we can ask them point-blank questions such as, "What caused you to say/do that? What is your reason?" We can ask them why they distract other students, what they hope to accomplish by doing so, what they hope to accomplish in life, who they feel they can sit by and not become a distraction to (or be distracted themselves), what they can do in place of acting silly, and we can even distract them by asking them about their day/interests/outfit/supplies, etc. Let's get to know these students who've come to us with this label, and let's help them outgrow it instead of owning it. If students are funny yet display it at inappropriate times, we could look for ways to provide them this outlet.

CLIP CHART

Public behavior charts of any kind shame students. Some are called "clip charts" because students' names are on spring-loaded clothesline pins, and they are either tacked onto the green (for good behavior) section, yellow (which signals a warning), or red (which equals trouble). Personally, if my name was moved to the yellow zone, it would make me angry. This, to me, is similar to the idea of dunce caps we'd see in very old photos in books or magazines. Shaming doesn't always *teach*. Clip charts can go by the wayside once we start talking with students one-on-one and explaining actions and consequences. For tips on how to manage the classroom, follow Elizabeth Merced (@EMercedLearning) and the hashtag #ditchtheclips on Twitter. The *Education Leadership* article "Tear down Your Behavior Chart!" offers a thorough look at why we need to ditch clip charts.
Read it here: bit.ly/WSclipchart.

COMPLAINT

Everyone has complaints. But do we need to voice them? Complaints, more often than not, are discussed with people who have no power to improve the situation. Many a lunch hour is spent complaining in the teacher's lounge. What happens after lunch? Most of the time, not much—if anything—because the people we are complaining to can't solve the problem we're facing. If, however, we take our complaints—*along with a possible solution*—to the source, there is a chance of something being done about it. That's one step closer to not having that same complaint ever again.

If the people around you have a habit of complaining, read Angela Watson's post, **"12 Ways to Deal with Chronic Complainers at Work" (bit.ly/WScomplaint)**.

COMPLIANCE

Compliance is something we often strive for. It often looks as if students are learning, or at the very least working on skills from our lesson. What's the next step? It's most likely engagement. In action, this looks like students are not only working, but *enjoying* their work. If we are able to move from compliance to engagement, we may be able to begin to *empower* our students. Seth Godin takes it even one step further and asks us to help students *contribute*: **bit.ly/WScontribute**.

CONFERENCING

"Conferencing," a word that has become popular lately, is used by educators to describe their one-on-one time chatting with students about their learning. A conference is a noun that we've been turning into a verb. We don't *conference* with students; we *confer*. Conferring is such a valuable practice, let's try to confer one-on-one with students every day.

CONTROL

There are only so many things we can control. One of my husband's favorite quotes is from Charles Swindoll (it's one of my favorites now, too): "The longer I live, the more I realize the impact of attitude on life . . . The only thing we can do is play on the one string we have, and that is our attitude . . . I am convinced that life is 10 percent what happens to me and 90 percent how I react to it."

Students, parents, peers, and administrators will behave in ways that we simply cannot control. How we respond in those situations can make the difference between being dragged through the muck and mire of an ugly encounter and rising above it. Our reactions can

15

define people's perceptions of us. We cannot control all situations. Rather than trying to control students, let's use our power and position to uncover their needs and support them.

See also: "manage"

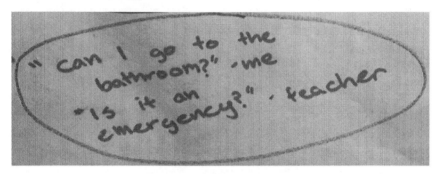

"CAN I GO TO THE BATHROOM?"—ME
"IS IT AN EMERGENCY?"—TEACHER

COUNTDOWN

I personally do not do countdowns when it comes to winter break, spring break, summer break . . . most years. We have students at our schools who would rather be at school than at home. For these children, school is a safe place, it's where they feel loved, and it's where they know they will eat at least once a day. For those children, our countdowns can cause them anxiety. Yes!!

If we're going to count down to something, let's make it a special day of celebration, a fun school event, or even the start of school after a break. Let's show students we want to be with them. Let's show them we enjoy this profession we chose. ✓

Full disclosure: I do count down to Friday on the especially tough weeks, but I do so only in my head. Out loud, on Monday, I let students know that I am thankful they are back. (I may even hang a sign saying, "Welcome back!") And then I try to make the days *count*.

CRAZY (AS A LABEL)

Some teachers and students hear someone calling them "crazy," and they own it! I've been there; I've done that. The word "crazy" can also have a negative connotation to it. My classroom ideas have been called "crazy" (by a parent), and I took it as an offense.

I'd like for educators to think of those crazy teachers who are trying different things in the classroom, or those students who do things differently from others, as "innovative," "thoughtful," "curious," "courageous," and, if their "crazy" ideas pan out, "impactful."

I've also called students "crazy" or "nuts," and, looking back, think of it as so very wrong. I could call them "creative," "inventive," or even "original."

On My Blog: **"Here's to the Crazy Ones": bit.ly/WScrazy**

DEMERIT

"Demerit" is an old-school term that is (thankfully) falling out of use. I don't hear it much these days, except for when I forget something and my husband says, "That's one demerit." When I searched Google for the definition, here's what I found: "a mark awarded against someone for a fault or offense." First, the word "awarded" threw me off. Next, I thought of the idea of a blank slate. If we are "awarding" marks against students (or colleagues), when do they ever get another clean slate again? Let's rid our language of demerits at school once and for all and start fresh with one another each day.

See also: "this group"

DENY

When I think of this word, I think of being denied some type of food. Sometimes it's ice cream; sometimes it's chocolate. Whatever it is, it's never a good feeling. Teachers deny students various privileges, some parents are denied their rights to their children, some teachers are denied funds, etc. No one likes to be denied something they want.

Let's try to "empower" one another. Let's empower one another as professionals. Let's empower our students as learners. Let's empower *ourselves*. Once we realize all that we can do, there should be no stopping us—if we believe it is right and good for our students.

See also: "just a _____ (teacher)"

DO THIS (AS A COMMAND)

Students (and teachers) don't like to be told what to do. When you offer a choice, however, people feel a sense of autonomy and may be more inclined to attempt the task. Try using the words "you choose" instead of "do this."

DO NOT/DON'T (AS A COMMAND)

"Don't" as a command may well be taken as a dare. Consider another teacher telling you not to do something. If you're anything like me, it might make you want to do it, just to say you *did*. Yikes!

Even if our students want to follow instructions, telling them what you *don't* want them to do can cause confusion. When you say, "Don't run!" the last word children hear is *run!* If you don't want children to do something, try saying what you do want them to do, like "walk." In the same way, rather than saying things like, "Don't touch each other," or "Don't touch his stuff," try saying, "Keep your hands to yourself."

And let's stop saying, "Don't touch!" If you're going to bring things to school for children to see, it is inevitable that children are going to touch them. It's in their nature. Try this: Leave it at home if you don't want it touched.

EASY

You may think a task is easy. It may not be easy for some of our peers or students.

See "simple"

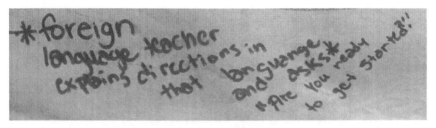

FOREIGN LANGUAGE TEACHER EXPLAINS DIRECTIONS IN THAT LANGUAGE AND ASKS
"ARE YOU READY TO GET STARTED?"

EXCEPT

Let's not leave anyone or anything out. Let's leave everything on the table, at least at the beginning of a decision-making process. What if, instead, we *accept* all we can? What if we leave all of our options open? Consider the possibilities!

EXTRA CREDIT

If students don't do well on work in the first place, wouldn't they learn more if they actually tried it *again*? Rick Wormeli, a middle school educator and the author of *Fair Isn't Always Equal*, calls extra credit a "grading malpractice." I can see his point. As a student, if I've done all the classwork to the best of my ability, I would think the teacher was being totally unfair if another student, who didn't do as much, was able to earn extra points for bringing in a ticket stub to a school show or a signed sheet or box of tissues! Check out a bit of Rick Wormeli's work here: **bit.ly/WSec1**. If you are still not convinced, I've gone on and on about various situations in this blog post: **bit.ly/WSextra**.

FAD

Fads come and go. Student fads, including bottle-flipping, fidget spinners, and Fortnite dances, come with a wave of popularity then fade out of memory. In the professional education world, I have a feeling we throw around the word "fad" too much when it comes to ideas educators are trying and sharing widely and wildly.

Rather than dismissing a popular idea as a "fad" (I remember when genius hour and gamification were "fads"), let's ask first *why* it began. What is all this intense, wild enthusiasm about? Why did the idea take off? Then let's check out the iterations to see how this idea can be used with students similar to ours. Does it fit in with what we're already doing? With that information and insight, it may turn out that the idea is useful to us too. We might even decide to change our entire teaching day due to our belief in the reasons *why* we need to be on the bandwagon of a current idea!

FAIL

"Fail" should not always have a negative connotation. If you type F.A.I.L. into a Google search bar, you'll see that some teachers use this word as an acronym to promote persistence and progress: "First Attempt In Learning." Another positive spin on the word is when we tell learners to "fail early and responsibly." The message: Try again. Let's encourage students to try, again and again, without risk of harmful failure.

Failure may result in a burst of ego or a gigantic mess; it doesn't mean we are doomed. We should learn from failing and not make that mistake again. I like to see failure as a bit of an experiment. If one thing fails, try it a different way. And what's the difference between using the words "failure" and "failing"? Check out A.J. Juliani's quick explanation in his video here: **bit.ly/WSfail**.

FEEDBACK *"Feedforward" - (next step?)*

Feedback, as a concept, is valuable. I once heard the term "feedforward." That made a ton more sense to me. Instead of looking *back* at what students have done (or not done), let's ask them to reflect then take the next step. We can help them set a goal for the next time. Once they have a goal, we can let them figure out two to three steps toward achieving that goal, but nothing huge (our brains can't handle too much at one time). Plan out small steps that they can take without much guidance; this can go a long way toward them applying this step-by-step plan on a new task. One takeaway I had from reading Joe Hirsch's *The Feedback Fix* was that too much negative feedback can shut down the learner. Consider sharing options with students as to where to go next. I've collected myriad resources in an online binder so we can provide more effective feedforward. Check out the subtabs under "How to Give Feedback" here: **bit.ly/WSgrades**.

FINE

A coworker and I have a challenge when we see each other in the hallways at school. When asked, "How are you?" we come up with a more precise word than "fine" to describe how we're feeling. I love this challenge—especially if I'm not quite awake yet when we meet! One thing I've noticed, however, is that I use many synonyms for "great," and I'm still not being very specific. Did you know that "great," "wonderful," "fantastic," "fabulous," and "stupendous" are all the same sign in American Sign Language? It's time for me to be more specific when someone asks, "How are you?"

A big focus in schools has been on social-emotional learning. This includes the practice of naming how we're feeling. Dr. Marc Brackett, from the Yale Center for Emotional Intelligence, has created the RULER approach. The first step, the "R" in RULER, stands for

20

recognizing emotion. "Fine" just doesn't cut it. Consider words that are more precise to explain how you truly are at that moment and use the words in front of peers and students. If needed, explain why you chose that particular word. Be the role model, so students can better recognize and express how they're feeling at any given point in time. Dr. Brackett's "mood meter" considers "energy" and "pleasantness." Students show in some fashion (on a bulletin board, in an electronic poll, etc.) how much energy and pleasantness they feel. I've found it difficult to explain "pleasantness" to students, yet they don't seem to mind, and they can fairly quickly assess how "pleasant" they feel at any particular moment. Some more precise words for students and colleagues to use in naming how they're feeling:

21

At Ease	Blissful	Alienated	Annoyed
Blessed	Cheerful	Alone	Apprehensive
Calm	Delighted	Apathetic	Distressed
Carefree	Ecstatic	Ashamed	Enraged
Chill	Elated	Bored	Flummoxed
Content	Energized	Disappointed	Frightened
Cool	Hyper	Disgusted	Frustrated
Fulfilled	Inspired	Down	Fuming
Grateful	Joyful	Drained	Furious
Harmonious	Jubilant	Embarrassed	Irate
Humble	Lively	Excluded	Livid
Relaxed	Motivated	Glum	Nervous
Relieved	Pleasant	Mopey	Peeved
Restful	Proud	Mortified	Repulsed
Satisfied	Surprised	Perplexed	Restless
Secure	Thrilled	Rattled	Troubled
Serene	Upbeat	Timid	Shocked
Tranquil	Optimistic	Tired	Uneasy

You can learn more about Marc Brackett's RULER approach and his mood meter at **bit.ly/WSfeelings**.

FIX

Please, please continue to try and fix problems. Fix that bookshelf that keeps tilting. Fix that thermostat that makes the room too cold. When it comes to people, however, stop trying to "fix" them. People aren't "broken." They don't need to be "fixed." They are most likely struggling, so let's consider what challenges they are dealing with and either try to help them cope with it or walk alongside them. Be aware that some struggles may be ongoing. We may think of having certain students in our classroom as a challenge for us. The students, however, may have a bigger challenge of trying to overcome struggles of which we're not even aware. Let's be there to support and guide them. Instructional coach and reading specialist Peg Grafwallner wrote about the words "struggling" and "reluctant" and suggests we use "developing" instead in her post: **bit.ly/WSfix**. We are all developing skills throughout life.

FIXED MINDSET ♡ Growth Mindset

Some students have a fixed mindset about certain areas in their lives; teachers often have a fixed mindset as well. Carol Dweck, PhD, researcher and author of the book *Mindset*, says that a fixed mindset means we believe our basic abilities, intelligence, and talents are fixed traits, meaning they cannot be improved. As we shift the language to incorporate more of a growth mindset (belief that abilities, intelligence, and talent can grow based on hard work, learning, and training), let's focus on those words and ideas—hard work, learning, and practice—not simply the term "growth mindset." When we reflect and notice improvements, let's encourage more of that hard work, learning, practice, persistence, and courage, so we can see further success in our students and in ourselves.

GAME-CHANGER (AS A LABEL FOR A TECH TOOL)

Via Tom McMurray (@thomascmurray) "We need to stop calling tools, apps, etc. 'game changers' in education. If your 'game' is technology-led, you're in the wrong park. Tech is a tool . . . an amplifier, not a desired pedagogical outcome. #CUE18."

22

Power of yet!

GENIUS (AS A LABEL)

Please explain this word if you're going to use it. Please do not have "Genius Hour" if not *all* of your students can participate. All students have genius—it's up to us to try to discover it in them, draw it out, and help them use it. I love Paul Solarz's idea of the Marble Theory that he shares in his book *Learn Like a Pirate*. He explains that we are all born with the same amount of marbles. Some of us allocate them to academics, some sports, some with a bit in each.

I believe part of our job is to find out where our students are currently housing their marbles. Let's get to know our learners so we can spot their genius, name it, and use it in classrooms where students can teach one another!

One way to learn to spot the genius in others is to first ask ourselves: *What is my genius?* Angela Maiers asked me this once, and I've realized my answer changes as I grow older. Contemplate that question a bit, then ask it of your students. We all have "genius" in us; let's help our students build on their particular genius.

More thoughts on the word in my blog post titled "Genius" here: **bit.ly/WSgenius.**

23

GIFTED (AS A LABEL)

Aren't all of our students gifted and talented in different ways? We can offer "accelerated" courses or courses with more "advanced" material, without putting labels on students. Once a student sees himself as "gifted," when things get tough, he may simply give up. In his head, he's supposed to know things. After all, he's "gifted." In my mind, labeling a child "gifted" makes being "normal" something negative. Consider how "gifted" classes are viewed. Are "normal" or "typical" classes less rigorous? Perhaps less productive? This is dependent on so many factors, such as which teacher is in the room and even how many students are in the room. Once we use this label of "gifted" or even "accelerated," we're also labeling the other courses unfairly. See more ideas here, from Sue Weinstein, author and associate professor at Louisiana State University: **bit.ly/WSgifted.**

GIVE UP (TIME)

So many times, we "sacrifice" or "give up" our time to activities beyond our control: an assembly to listen to the chorus and band students, a school-wide sing-along in the gym, a "walk of fame" or parade during the day to celebrate an achievement or a team. Let's not use the phrase "give up" when talking about the time that is shifting to these activities.

Try thinking and using the word "invest" instead. When we invest time beyond the confines of our lesson plans with students, they realize that school is not solely about academics. School is about learning, for sure. Learning, however, includes discovering how to build relationships, make connections, work as a team, play fairly, and celebrate others.

It's been said (and proven, in my own experience attending school) our students won't really remember what we teach. They will remember *how* we teach. I hope they remember that we care, investing time in what we believe students should learn beyond the pre-scripted academic curriculum.

GOSSIP

It's so easy to do. Talking about others seems natural in the school system. We talk about students—their strengths and struggles. We also talk about teachers—what they're doing, what they're not doing, what we heard them say, what students say they said, etc.

All that talk leads to gossip, plain and simple. Gossip, used as a noun or a verb, does nothing positive for us. When you hear an educator begin to gossip, choose to say something nice to defend the person they're talking about. If you cannot say anything nice, consider walking away from the conversation. Stopping a gossip session will help you feel better about the person being talked about and about yourself. Refusing to listen to gossip frees you from being burdened with the "bad stuff" about your colleagues (stuff which may or may not be true), and your relationship with them will be better than if you had heard any gossip.

GRADE GRUBBERS (AS A LABEL)

Teachers have perpetuated a system in which many students want good grades. Parents have put pressure on their children for decades. Yes, students will continue to try to get more points where they can, as long as we are using a traditional form of grading. The word "grub" has a negative label that literally means an insect or its larva. Our students are looking for more points and good grades due to years of adults telling them that's how to succeed in school.

GRADES/MARKS/POINTS

Sometimes teachers use marks or points as leverage for students to work. Let's make the move toward "learning" and "improvement." Of course, this word-choice shift is much easier to do and works better if you have *no* grades or points. If you do use points, consider not averaging them all together for one grade. Consider using only the most recent evidence—not their past learning and mistakes averaged with it.

Once you start including activities in class that do not have points or marks attached, you'll want every lesson and activity to be more relevant to your students. When you are able to make learning relevant, the language changes, and you can focus on the learning students are doing and the importance of the work, without mention of points, marks, percentages, and letter grades.

Check the "Teacher Journeys" tab in the "Feedback in Lieu of Grades" LiveBinder for stories from teachers who do not use marks/points in schools that still do expect an end-of-term letter grade: **bit.ly/WSgrades**.

GREAT JOB

This phrase sounds solid. We can make it better by either following up with specifics, or simply starting with specifics. Consider focusing on what, exactly, was so great. In physical education, you could say, "Your focus was spot on! It looks like you put a lot of effort into that lap!" In music, try something like, "You're reading the notes more accurately." At lunch, compliments like, "Your area was spotless today!" can go a long way. Tell people (students and colleagues) what they are doing well—specifically—so they can continue to progress.

GROW STUDENTS

I've seen this quote many times (attributed to many authors, mostly Alexander Den Heijer): "When a flower doesn't bloom, you change the environment in which it's in, not the flower." This quote may make educators think of their students as flowers, and some teachers may want to "grow students" who are kind, patient, etc. Children are not flowers, however. Children are moving all around, not firmly planted in any one spot. Consider "helping them grow," "guiding their growth," or "nurturing students," but not growing them.

GROW UP

I teach twelve-year-olds. I often think I want them to grow up. *C'mon, just be more mature, won't you?* Nope. They actually can't—yet. They have the brain of a twelve-year-old, the body of a child somewhere between eight and fourteen years old, and hormones to boot. Let's enjoy the awkward ages of twelve, thirteen, or even six or sixteen. Let's allow them to be the age they are; they grow up all too quickly without us pushing them.

See also: "man up"

GRUDGE

I hold grudges all the time. I am working on stopping this habit, and it's a hard one to break.

Grudges, large or small, affect our daily lives. They may be held consciously or subconsciously. They may be a result of something that has happened to us in the past or based on gossip. Sometimes we hold a grudge against people simply because they remind us of someone else.

We can prevent some grudges by staying away from negative language or gossip. But when we become aware of them in our lives, we can work on freeing ourselves from them. Yes, grudges are difficult to "get over," but the longer we hold a grudge, the more it poisons us from the inside. Find something positive about that person you feel an animosity toward. Get to know that person a little better. Find something you have in common with that person and get to work on repairing any damage. It's harmful to us (mentally, which could lead to physical effects) if we do not let those negative feelings go.

GUYS

Times are changing, for sure! Having transgender students in classes has made me notice my students' and my own language and helped me have a more gender-neutral vocabulary. I've grown up in a different world from our students, and I've grown used to seating my students with a mix of males and females at each table. I've stopped splitting students by gender (boys on one side and girls on another), yet I still sometimes use the word "guys" when addressing an entire group. I now have to be aware of who I'm excluding with the word "guys." Some may not care, yet some may see it as disrespectful. It could also be troubling for those students in our classes who are transitioning; not using this word is one more way of showing care and respect. **Here's more from The Atlantic:** bit.ly/WSguys.

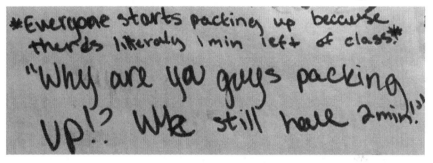

EVERYONE STARTS PACKING UP BECAUSE THERE'S LITERALLY 1 MIN LEFT OF CLASS.
"WHY ARE YOU GUYS PACKING UP?! WE STILL HAVE 2 MIN!"

HACK

I always imagine an ax when I hear this word—or, better yet, the movie *Hush . . . Hush, Sweet Charlotte* (Bette Davis supposedly "hacked off his hand and head"!). Hackers try to get into people's accounts. Hackers make things stop functioning the way they were intended. It's got such a negative connotation to it that maybe it should only be used for negative behaviors. Instead of using "hack," I try using the words "tweak" or "improve."

HANDLE KIDS THAT . . .

Teachers often ask one another, "How do you handle kids that continue talking when you are? How do you handle kids that _____?"

Let's rethink that phrase. We're not "manipulating" the kids, nor should we be "managing" them. Handlers train animals, and sometimes they need to use force.

Alternatives to the questions could include phrases like, "What do you do about kids that _____?" This slight shift in words shows more courtesy toward students and may even help our mindset when we are helping each other answer these tough questions.

HATERS (AS A LABEL)

They probably don't really hate you. You may annoy them. They could simply be jealous. They may be jealous of the happiness you have (or appear to have).

When people speak negatively about us or even try to sabotage our work, let's choose to take it as a learning opportunity. *How can we respond to those people in a way that makes us feel justified and also leaves them asking questions or reflecting?* (After an altercation such as this, you might share that story—protecting names, of course—and more importantly what you learned from it.) Use what you've learned from the "haters" to be proactive for the next time by giving them the same attention and attitude you show others. Be proud of what you're doing and share your reasons why. You'll then be better able to better defend yourself against the next instance of negativity.

This word is inspired by Taylor Swift's song "Shake It Off."

HAVE TO

"Do I *have to*?" Thinking about how many times I said this in my younger years makes me a little queasy. Even so, I catch myself telling students, "We have to get this done today," or "We have to take this test to show our growth."

Saying "have to" makes what we're doing sound like it's work. Can we substitute "get to" instead? Funny enough, when I apply the phrase "get to," even if I don't really want to, such as saying, "I get to wash the car," I actually end up liking the task a little better!

28

Using "get to" makes it sound like an opportunity. If it doesn't feel like an opportunity, this is our opportunity to change the activity to make it more relevant to ourselves and our students. If we cannot control the activity, let's find a way to make it useful to students. In other words, look for and share the reasons why you "get to" do certain activities. If your students don't catch on to this shift in your words, you can show them author Jon Gordon's quick motivational video here: **bit.ly/WShaveto**.

HIGH (AS A LABEL)

We often find ourselves ranking our students. "My high group" may have higher scores on tests overall. My "high" students may struggle with . . . well . . . struggle itself. They may struggle when it comes to getting anything other than an "A" for a grade. As soon as I call them my "high" group, even in my head, I tend to treat the entire group differently. I may assume too much. I may set the bar too high, without enough scaffolds available for them. I may make the task "too" open-ended. I begin to make assumptions that may or may not be correct. Instead of clumping students in one group, I could look at exactly where they excel, then use that skill to hook them up with other students who could use some guidance, support, or modeling. Let's look for specific strengths, such as perseverance, creativity, and adaptability, then let them know the specific skills we've noticed so they can use them for further progress and learning.

HOLD STUDENTS ACCOUNTABLE

As an opponent of typical grading systems, I often hear that "zeroes hold students accountable." I've heard that zeroes "teach responsibility." Instead of holding our students accountable, let's teach them how to act as responsible citizens. When they fail at it, let's ask them to reflect on what happened, and how they'd change it for next time. And then . . . one more step . . . let's provide the opportunity for students to try it again. We are still holding them accountable, but with less of a power trip for us and more of an opportunity for their further learning.

HOMELESS (AS A LABEL)

My lot in life used to be a "traveling teacher." I taught deaf and hard-of-hearing students throughout the county for five years, so I kept everything I needed for each day in my pickup truck (An all-manual Mitsubishi Mighty Max!). I understand what it feels like not to have a permanent teaching space in the school you work in. I understand what it's like to have five different mailboxes and still not receive any notice that the students have an assembly when I show up. Even with that understanding, I feel a little sick when I hear teachers say they "have no home" or are "homeless" at school. Is it fair to compare your lot in your school district to people who don't have shelter—a place of their own to eat or sleep? Some genuinely homeless people live in our neighborhoods or surrounding areas. You may have students who truly know what it means to live without food or a warm bed.

If you want more than an office space, a desk in "someone else's" room, a closet for your supplies, or your car if you travel, look for another teaching position. Or continue to work in the same position, figuring out how to make your time and space more useful. Whatever setting you're in, you can still give the children in your care your very best.

30

HOMEWORK

To some people, *not* using this word feels radical. Homework is a tradition; it's the way school has been done for decades. Perhaps some see homework assignments as an "opportunity for learning" or "independent practice." But even when we have the best of intentions, homework isn't all it's cracked up to be. Current research reveals that most homework does not benefit students. Experience has shown that many homework assignments cause anxiety and arguments at home. Once we're analytical of exactly what we are expecting students to do outside school hours, we'll reconsider and tweak our expectations.

If we're going to expect students to do homework, let's make it relevant to them, provide a way for them to share it the next day in class, and provide time in class for the students to reflect on how they did. It should have an aspect of choice and student voice. One more thing: If you're still assigning "homework" (which should really be "practice" of skills practiced in class or "home learning," as podcaster and author Barbara Bray likes to use), keep it out of the gradebook.

For more information on why we need to stop with the homework, check out this bit of research here from Alfie Kohn: **bit.ly/WShomework**.

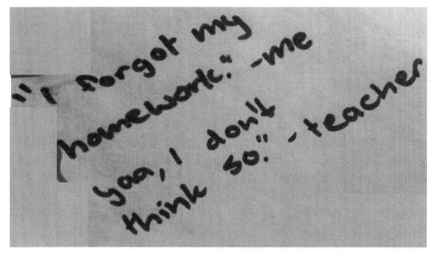

"I FORGOT MY HOMEWORK."—ME
"YAA, I DON'T THINK SO."—TEACHER

HURRY UP

Life goes by so fast as it is. I'm more inclined to "slow down" these days than I was early in my teaching career. Sometimes we just have to let things simmer. The end result is often more desirable.

I'M SORRY, BUT

My grandpa (Papa) used to say, "Don't say you're sorry." I didn't know what he meant for the longest time. Then I figured something out: If you're going to *say* "I'm sorry" while adding more afterward, try to avoid having to say you're sorry in the first place. When you do, please avoid saying the word "but" after.

See also: "but"

IMPOSSIBLE

I'm going to add another country song reference here: Joe Nichols' song "The Impossible" explains that even the strongest steel can bend, and even unsinkable ships can sink. We tell our students that they can do anything they choose to do, as long as they work hard enough at it (and have the right opportunities). What educators and administrators might deem to be "impossible" *can* actually happen if conditions are right. Try substituting "improbable," then ask students if they can prove you wrong. Imagine what would be *possible*...

IN THE TRENCHES

When I present at conferences, many attendees are happy because I'm still working in a school environment. They enjoy the fact that a teacher, still "in the trenches" (as they say), is sharing ideas and stories with them. I understand their position, as I, too, appreciate learning from someone else going through much of what I'm going through. This phrase simply leaves a bad taste in my mouth. Comparing ourselves to soldiers who fought for their country during various wars just isn't fair to our students, our communities, or our veterans. We have the opportunity to take a break, whereas they did not always have that chance. Instead of saying we're "in the trenches," let's consider stating that, yes, we are currently working in the educational system, and we have practical experience to share.

INCOMPETENT

I've heard teachers say this of other educators or administrators, and I've heard of teachers saying this to students. If we believe a *colleague* to be incompetent, we've got choices. We can go directly to the source and talk about the issue or even help that person develop the skills they need to succeed. We can collect evidence to provide for someone who should be alerted, or we can simply not give that person responsibilities that we could do better ourselves.

If we believe a *student* is incompetent at a certain skill, there is absolutely no need to share that belief with the student. If the child truly does not have the skills to do something successfully, we have work to do. Our next steps are to look at what necessary skills that student needs and then help them develop those skills.

Rather than calling a person "incompetent," let's use some of our own knowledge and help that person learn and grow. We too have been incompetent at various points in our lives (and will be again).

We became competent when someone (a mentor, coach, or teacher) helped us become successful. Such is the way of our profession. We help others to succeed. We help others become competent so they can continue to learn long after we're out of their lives. Let's take out the "in-" and simply do our best to help one another become more "competent."

YOU'RE INCOMPETENT.

INSTAGRAMMER/TWEETER (AS A LABEL)

Some classrooms have a "classroom Instagrammer" or "classroom tweeter." What is this person doing? Publicizing, sharing, self-promoting, connecting? Try "publicist" or "inquirer," or refer to that person as "one who contributes to conversations" or "one who shares the good in this world." The skill will develop as the user becomes more comfortable with the tools, and the tools will most likely change. Let's use the words that describe what the person is actually doing. Our students will most likely use them, as well, figuring out along the way what these definitions actually mean, and how their position contributes to our world of social media.

INTERVENTION

The word "intervention" sounds like it has a negative connotation. Many shows feature interventions for alcoholics or drug addicts. An intervention is technically an "action taken to improve a situation." Can we consider using "action to take" or "next steps" to describe how we'll try intervening?

JERK/A$$HOLE/INSERT ANY DEROGATORY NAME HERE (AS A LABEL, SAID IN PRIVATE)

I've done it. I've used derogatory names—not to anyone's face but behind their backs, out of earshot. More frequently, I've thought those words, even if I haven't said them aloud. That doesn't make me right. In fact, this truth about myself makes me feel sick to my stomach. I don't have the right to call anyone names, even in my thoughts.

There will be some days during the school year that you want to use harsh words to describe students or peers. Before you open your mouth, consider what happens when you hear a colleague speak ill of someone. Personally, when I hear someone call their students or coworkers something nasty, I suddenly think, *I wonder what she says about me when I'm not around?* My esteem for that person instantly goes down. Case in point: A while back, I met a woman at a neighborhood gathering. As we spoke, she used the nastiest name for her students. (I won't repeat it here—or anywhere.) Taken aback, I refrained from forming an opinion about her students, but I suddenly had a terrible opinion of her.

Once we attach a label to a person, we look for those characteristics in that person. Let's choose not to apply hurtful labels; let's look for the good. Let's keep the hope alive that our role modeling, attention, care, and love will help even the most frustrating people we know to lose their negative labels. It might not happen overnight—or ever—but that doesn't mean we can't try. Let's be the role model and have hope that people can learn.

One final note: In my opinion, if you've completely lost hope in people's ability to grow and change, it may be unfair to students if you continue teaching.

JOB

Jobs are normally paid positions. It helps to call classroom jobs "responsibilities," especially if you're letting students choose them. By doing so, the focus is on class community rather than work. The same goes for us as professionals. We are in the profession of teaching. For so many, it's not simply a job—it's a calling. "If it's something you love," as my dad has said, "you'll never work a day in your life."

34

I love to say teaching is my "profession." That also helps me treat it as such, so I continue learning as I teach, as other professionals do.

JUST A [TEACHER]

You are not "just" anything. You deserve respect. You are oftentimes a counselor, a parent, a mediator, a listener, a problem-solver, a contributor, a _____ (you fill in the blank). Joe Sanfelippo, superintendent and author of *Hacking Leadership*, shows his staff daily what they mean to their students. He thanks them personally and publicly, he shares the fabulous everyday successes with the world through his social media accounts, and he always gives his staff shout-outs when I'm fortunate enough to hear him speak in person. He knows we are not "just" teachers. We are so much more, and we should be proud of it.

Rather than *just a teacher*, I love the term Rick Wormeli, middle school teacher and author of *Fair Isn't Always Equal*, uses to describe educators: *highly-accomplished practitioners*. Yes! Be proud. Own it. Live it.

The words to try with "I am a _____" follow here: *reader, researcher, writer, contributor, explorer, collaborator, hypothesizer, experimenter, adventurer, risk-taker, learner, visionary, coach, guide, supporter, amplifier, leader, change-agent, difference-maker—hero*. How do we empower ourselves? By using these words and believing in them. A bit more from me in this quick video: **bit.ly/WSjusta**.

KIDS THESE DAYS

Our parents said it, and so did their parents. It's often used to describe a negative trend. If we're going to say, "kids these days," we might as well add "adults these days," as we're *all* different from how we were "back in the day." Kids these days are learning more than we ever could imagine when we were kids. They are waiting for relevance and wanting to work toward a purpose. Kids these days often do more than we give them credit for. They're our future. Let's talk about them and treat them with respect—as individuals rather than a homogenous group.

LATER

Schedule it. Let peers and students know it *will* happen. Show them you are listening and believe their ideas are valuable by responding and acting on them. I will use the word "later" only if I can schedule the activity and follow through. If you feel as if you truly want it to happen, try saying, "Let's schedule it." Put it on the calendar and share it with students and parents. When you do that, you won't put it off until *later*.

LAZY (AS A LABEL)

Let's substitute "demotivated" for this one. Or better yet, can we find out why we think a child appears to be lazy or not motivated? Become curious. Collect some data. This word generates more questions than answers. Keep asking the questions that keep these conversations going, no matter how futile it may seem during the school year. Where else do they act this way? When do they not act "lazy" or unmotivated?

When we have information, we are better equipped to help the student find his or her motivation. We can experiment with ways to make our lessons more relevant to that student.

LECTURE

There is a time and place for lectures in the classroom, to be sure. Try to "disseminate" or "present" information or "share"—and let's keep our own presenting to a minimum! The one talking is the one doing the learning. Let's have the learners present or share what they're learning. It's a blessing to see students leading their own learning by "disseminating," "presenting," or "sharing" information. (You can even do as Brian Durst, a high school English teacher, suggests and play students' self-selected "walk-on song" prior to sharing their ideas with the class.)

LET IT GO

Oh, I'm all about letting things go—particularly tension, stress, bad vibes, negativity, and even teacher control. ***See my blog post on that here:*** bit.ly/WSletitgo.

I'd like to challenge us to practice the idea behind another phrase: "Soak it up." Our students get off track, off task, off topic. Their inattention may make us upset for various reasons, and it has the potential to sidetrack our day. Sometimes we think, *I've got to let this go.* But what if we take the time, in that moment, to realize the stage of life our students are going through and instead choose to "soak it up"? By that, I mean soak up the humor of the moment, the development of the frontal lobe, the learning that will (hopefully) take place when you calmly redirect the behavior. Soak up the fact that students benefit from a teacher like you who understands that everyone learns at his or her own pace. Soak it up, soak it in, and immerse yourself in the moment so you can remember the experience when you're thinking of your fondest days of teaching long after you retire.

LOW (AS A LABEL)

"My low class" may have lower scores on tests overall. My "low" students may struggle with tasks in a specific subject area. Once I call them "low," even in my head, I might think of them in a negative light or develop a different perception of them. Again, I may make assumptions that simply are not true. I may not expect as much from them as I should. I may set the bar too low for them. I may make the task easier than they need it to be. Instead of clumping students in a group, I can look at exactly where they struggle, then pinpoint that aspect of their learning. In this fashion, I can help this group of students individually.

MAKE THEM

"You can lead a horse to water, but you can't make it drink." The same goes for people. Adults and children alike have their own agendas and intentions. If we're trying to "make" students do something, let's try to "encourage," "explain reasons why," and "model" how.

MAN UP

This phrase is akin to "grow up" but with a gender focus. Do we need to perpetuate the roles men and women have historically played? Do men have to be stronger or tougher than women? What might you say to a young lady that would mean the same thing?

What does it mean to "man up"? Instead of using this phrase, let's explain to young people the actions and behaviors we expect of them.

See also: "grow up"

MANAGE

To manage is to "be in charge of, administer, or run." Who runs your classroom? Many times, it's the students. (Who *should* be running our classrooms? Most times, it's the students.) Who runs what we do? It's mostly up to us. We can manage ourselves. Maybe we should let our students take on some of the management roles in our classrooms.

More often than not, I've found that when I trust students with responsibilities, they come through. When they don't, we all learn a lesson. We can then regroup, reassess, and make plans for improvement.

See Catlin Tucker's post about how she lets students lead more often and has few "management" issues: **bit.ly/WSmanage**.

See also: "control"

"SIT DOWN."

MARKS/GRADES/POINTS

I propose we move toward "learning" and "improvement."

See also: "grades"

MESSY

I do not like messes. The cardboard challenge, complete with cardboard, scissors, duct tape, and homemade decorations scattered around the room (for three classes, no less), is a tough week in our room—for me. I remember complaining about it during one of our team meetings, and a colleague said, "I thought you liked messy." I responded that I don't, but I believe the activity is right and good for my students.

A "messy" room can mean many things. It can mean things are not put away (for any number of reasons), it may mean it's actually dirty, or it may mean chaos to other students and teachers. If you want to use the word "messy," consider what is actually going on in the class and try to use those words instead. Are students creating? Collaborating? Working on student-driven learning? Engaged in discovery? If I had thought about what was actually going on in our "messy" classroom at the time, I probably wouldn't have complained about it in the first place. Also consider some wise words from educator and author Dave Mulder: **bit.ly/WSmessy**.

And if you don't yet know about the cardboard challenge, see **cainesarcade.com** for inspiration to try one at your own school.

MINION (AS A LABEL)

If you consider yourself the dominant power in the room, then your students just may be your "minions." If, however, you believe that all young learners in your presence add value to the learning experience for everyone in the room, consider calling them what they are: children. The children in my classroom are not servile or unimportant, nor are they my *underlings*, as the word "minion" implies outright. They are children, learners, and contributors to the classroom environment.

MISFIT (AS A LABEL)

I know I was a "misfit" in junior high. I could sense it. When I watched *Rudolph the Red-Nosed Reindeer* on television, I did not want to belong on the Island of Misfit Toys. They were, according to their song, "unwanted," and "one that no little boy or girl loves."

If mis = not, it is up to the adults to help all of our students fit. I will not accept that one student of mine does not fit. Let's take in these children, see where we can help them make connections with other children, and do our best to bring about feelings of inclusion and help them fit in somewhere.

MUFFIN (AS A LABEL)

Let's stop referring to our students as food. *Peanut,* (smart) *cookie, pork chop, pumpkin, hot dog,* etc. also fall into this category. How would you like to be called a "muffin?" How close is that to cupcake, which some people use to describe a woman's looks, or even to debase a male's sexuality? Check the list of positive labels at the end of this book for words we can encourage our students to live up to.

MUNCHKIN (AS A LABEL)

"Munchkin" means "a child" or "a short person," but it was derived from *The Wizard of Oz.* In Frank Baum's book, Dorothy thinks the munchkins in Oz are "the queerest people she had ever seen." I'm aware that most people might not be aware of this factoid, and our children might never look it up. But what if even just one knew the true meaning? There's no need to use this word to describe or label a child. Let's use the list of positive labels at the end of this book, so students have something to strive for.

MY

Try "our" when it fits the situation, as when talking about our school, our classrooms, and our students. The school and classrooms inside belong to our students, first and foremost. We have many "traveling" teachers in our profession, and we should be welcoming them to work with our students in *any* classroom in the school. When "my" room is being used during our lunch period, or when there's another teacher in "my" room during my personal planning time, I am aware that each room belongs to our students. Let's find ways to provide these students and teachers with space for their materials in each room as well.

When it comes to children, they're all *ours.* We do not walk the halls with blinders on, and we cannot only help or say hello to the students enrolled in our grade or courses. We are role models for all, and we should be sharing the responsibility of educating each child—inside and outside of our buildings.

NEGATIVITY

Instead of focusing on the negative (which our brains are wired to do), let's focus on the positive. Whatever we put in our minds is what we will continue to dwell upon. I have to tell myself this every day: *I did my best.* I have bad days like everyone else. Students sit in front of me disrespecting themselves and those around them by chatting or making loud noises. A child who was following me around one day is now shrugging her shoulders and not answering any question of mine the next. If I continue to list what could go wrong in a classroom, my blood pressure would rise, I may begin to get a headache, and this negativity would continue. If I choose instead to focus on what went well (we were able to get outside for a lesson, one child told me "thank you," or that class went better than expected), my attitude will stay mostly positive, and I can continue looking for and recognizing more positives the rest of my day. Try listing fifteen good things that happened each day and see how your attitude (and perhaps even your health) improves.

Check out this positive article from Mindshift, and end your days positively: **bit.ly/WSnegativity.**

NO

There are times we might need to say "no," such as when something isn't safe. Try "stop." Or when we are doing too much, try "not now." Consider questions you could ask instead of jumping right to "no" when students ask you a question. Questions that could work:

- Is it safe?
- Is it respectful?
- Is now a good time?
- Why not? (< my personal favorite)

The more I say "no" to students, the more I realize they do not have the same opportunities to say "no" to me. Associate Professor of Educational Leadership at the University of Colorado Denver and author Scott McLeod explains this issue of being able to say "no" very frankly in this post: **bit.ly/WSsayingno.**

NON-RACIST

We hope that our children and students are "non-racist," yet we can go a step further. Let's be—and encourage them to be—*anti-racist*.

Seek out great literature and learn from others who model forthright discussions about race with students. I do not consider myself knowledgeable enough to share more of my own thoughts here, so I encourage you to check out this quick and powerful post about being "anti-racist": **bit.ly/WSnonracist**. Then, especially if you're white like me, check out books like the ones on this very limited list for additional insight:

- *Blindspot: Hidden Biases of Good People* by Mahzarin Banaji and Anthony Greenwald
- *So You Want to Talk about Race* by Ijeoma Oluo
- *Things That Make White People Uncomfortable* by Michael Bennett
- *Waking up White and Finding Myself in the Story of Race* by Debby Irving
- *White Fragility: Why It's So Hard for White People to Talk about Racism* by Robin DiAngelo
- *Why I'm No Longer Talking to White People about Race* by Reni Eddo-Lodge

NOT ENOUGH TIME

We will never have "enough" time. Instead of dwelling on the time we do *not* have, let's look at the few minutes we do have with students and practice the word "prioritize." Let's prioritize the time we do have and implement what's best for our current students. In doing so, we will model for students what we value.

If, after prioritizing your time in class, you still feel that you do not have enough time, check out Angela Watson's 40-hour work week club: **40htw.com/join**. I signed up for her free five-day challenge by responding to her "Goodbye Teacher Tired" invitation. The tips I implemented from the challenge helped me to chunk tasks throughout my day so I could make better use of my time.

NUTS/CRAZY

I've had students in the past whom I've called "nuts" or "crazy," then followed up with "takes one to know one," meaning I was the same as them. Then came the school year when I had a student who had a mother with mental illness, whom she barely knew because she was in a home. At one point, she said to a peer, "My mom is nuts. No. Literally." This made me see how not funny it was to her when someone called a classmate or teacher "nuts" or "crazy."

If we want to show students we love their quirks, let's say things such as, "I love to do that, too," "I'm like you when I'm around my own friends," "I love your energy/vibe/attitude," or "Your creativity/imagination makes me smile."

At other times, ideas I've tried in my classroom have been called "crazy." Some educators may own it. I do not. I'd rather the ideas be called "out-of-the-box" or "innovative." I've piloted supposedly "crazy" ideas (Genius Hour, no grades) that have turned out to be revolutionary in my own classes and school. Share the successes and failures of ideas you're trying. If you can get enough educators on board, suddenly your "crazy" ideas will become the norm—and may even become what is expected in education in our era.

43

OVERWHELMED

Let's not let our workload and stress level get this far. What were the precursors to us saying we're "overwhelmed"? When I'm feeling as if our profession is a bit much, I think about buckling up for a ride on a plane. The announcement comes on to share how to use the oxygen masks. "Apply your own mask before helping those around you." In the same way, I say to you (and to myself), "Teachers, take care of yourselves so you can take care of the students."

Let's be on the lookout—in ourselves and in others—for hints at this word popping up. Let's squash "overwhelm" before it becomes a reality. Hopefully we will be able to say, "I'm living a more balanced life" more often.

Author Angela Watson provides four feasible self-care tips for educators in this interview with Jennifer Gonzalez: **bit.ly/WSoverwhelmed**.

Also, check out educator and author Dan Tricarico's books, *The Zen Teacher* and *Sanctuaries*.

PARENTS SHOULD

"Parents should have to take a test before they can have children." I've heard a few educators in my life say this. And, yes, I'm guilty of uttering those words myself in the past. (*How I wish I had a delete button for my words sometimes!*) Who are we to say a test should decide *anything*, much less whether two people should have children? We do not know what parents do or do not do at home. We also don't know what influences them, what they've gone through, or what they're currently going through. I don't think it's fair to talk about parents and the things they *should* be doing. Each family has its own way of operating. Let's hear from them when something is not working. Let's try to put our minds and ideas together to help make life better for them and their children.

PENALTY

When it comes to late work, many teachers enact a late work "penalty." This could be points off, a certain percentage off, or possibly even a zero for the assignment. What if we changed the language to a *consequence* instead? Granted, as an adult with the responsibility of paying for things like a mortgage, it's true that if I do not pay a bill on time, I may have to pay an extra "penalty fee." This has happened to me before, when I lost the bill or I thought it may never have come in the mail. Afraid of the penalty, I called the credit card company and explained my situation. As it was my "first offense," they waived the fee. The consequence? I learned the fear that came with a threat of a penalty and put it on my calendar the next month to make sure I paid on time. The other consequence? I was suddenly more lenient with my students; I didn't want to put fear in them if they were late turning in a paper in my language arts classes. I still have due dates, but now, if they forget to turn it in or they take extra time on it, it's no problem for me. I've got enough student work to look through. Sure, the grade book (or narrative feedback) remains empty until they get it in. No biggie.

I realize that in some classes, punctuality is necessary. If a student's work is late or missing, consider having that student see you first thing after school or first thing the next morning to get this work to you or, if nothing else, create the time for that student to complete the work. If this student continues to turn work in late, consider having him or her stay after each day to complete their assignments. Also consider what type of organizational tools or strategies will help them turn things in on time.

Let's try to stop using penalties to demonstrate our power. Let's see (and share with students) what kind of natural consequences occur when an assignment is late. Perhaps they didn't learn the information in time for the assessment. Or maybe, because they took more time to turn it in, they don't get a chance to revise. If they're late repeatedly, it's time to have a discussion and make a plan of action—with consequences defined.

POINTS/GRADES/MARKS

I propose we move toward "learning" and "improvement."

See also: "grades"

45

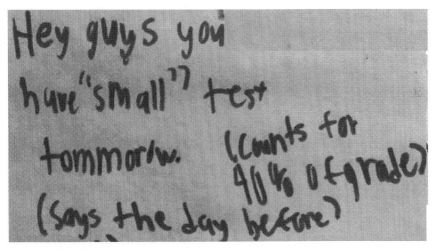

HEY GUYS YOU HAVE A 'SMALL' TEST TOMORROW. (COUNTS FOR 40% OF GRADE)
(SAYS THE DAY BEFORE)

POP QUIZ

We need to stop ambushing students. Pop quizzes are stressful "got-cha" moments for our learners. Students' trust in us will diminish or be eliminated altogether. If you must check for understanding (which is something I feel we need to be doing to see where to go next with our plans), try "comprehension check," "exit slip," "reflection," or ask students to "show what you know." Of course, these checks and reflections do not go in the grade book. Formative assessments such as these show the teacher if they should slow down or keep going, or who to reteach.

PRODUCE STUDENTS WHO . . .

We are long past the years of the factory model of schooling—or at least we should be. Why are we still "producing" students? The children in our schools were produced (aka created) years ago. We are trying to guide, lead, and encourage them.

PUNISH

Punishing students is supposed to be one way to teach students right from wrong. If all we want is compliance from students, then punishing may be one route to take. My bet, however, is that we want students to be engaged in relevant learning that will make a difference in their lives. If we punish students by putting them in the hall, is that shaming them? If we punish students with an out-of-school suspension, will they enjoy the time at home? What lessons will they miss? I have another question for those at schools where corporal punishment still exists: Where are your success stories? Let's work on repairing relationships. If students are acting out, let's help them see why it's a disturbance to the class, reflect on what happened and why, and make a plan for moving forward.

I love this viewpoint on restorative discipline from Carla Meyrink, founder of The Community for Learning School: **bit.ly/WSpunish**.

Learn even more from former elementary teacher Carla Shalaby's book *Troublemakers*.

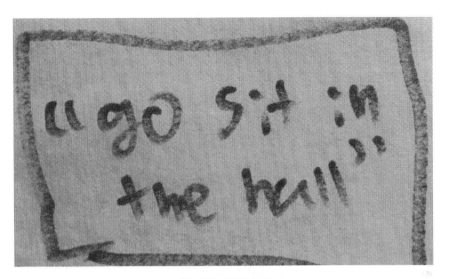

"GO SIT IN THE HALL."

QUITTER (AS A LABEL)

I've probably called a student of mine a "quitter," thinking it was motivation for them to keep going. *Ha!* More than likely, they'll live up to that label.

Part of the definition of a "quitter" is "a person who gives up easily." How do we know how much effort a person is putting into something? We may have a vague idea or think we know. That doesn't mean we're right by any means.

Instead of calling students—or colleagues—quitters, let's help them stay the course. Let's lead them to success, one bit at a time. If they express that they do not want to continue, let's have that conversation about the reasons why, help them reflect on what steps they've already taken, and make plans from there. It just may be that it is time for that person to quit that task, and we hadn't yet a clue what was going on prior to our discussion. If the child decides to continue, let's use words such as "perseverance," "courage," and "determination."

REGRET

This is such a backward-looking word—with seemingly no solutions. I wish we didn't have regrets. Instead of having regrets, let's try doing what we believe to be the right thing each and every day. When there are decisions to make, we often know in our heart what is right and what is not. Let's not procrastinate taking opportunities that come our way. Instead, let's venture into the unknown realm when an opportunity presents itself. Let's use the word "welcome" when we hear of opportunities. In doing so, we will greet the learning that comes our way as not-to-be-missed opportunities.

RETIRE

Yes. I talk about it. I'm twenty-four years in. I wonder. I keep watching those educators around me getting younger and younger. And yet, I have those awesome days when my students surprise me with all they can do, the questions they ask one another, the guidance and respect they provide one another, and I know I'm in the right profession. If you're thinking of retiring, of course get those papers and funds in order. Next, search for hashtags for what you love about teaching on your favorite social media tool. Connect with educators and get inspired once more. Then soak up all the learning and enjoy reaping the rewards of the effect your new-found invigoration will have on your students. When it's time to use the word "retire," I'll bet we'll know.

See also: "Let it go"

RISK

Unless there is real danger involved, try looking at a supposed "risk" as a *chance* or *opportunity*. Many of the things that educators call "risky" truly are not. When we experiment with different ideas in the classroom, it can be called "scientific inquiry" or even "action research." Even if the idea isn't the greatest, we can then reflect and share our findings with others, so they can learn from our own adventures in learning. When it turns out to be a great idea, we can reflect, share our findings, ask for further feedback, then tweak it so it works even better next time.

See also: "regret"

ROGUE

Some teachers use the word "rogue" to define their teaching. "I'm going rogue!" First, when we use it like this, it's no longer a noun.

One definition of this word is "dishonest or unprincipled person." Synonyms include "con artist," "crook," "swindler," and "villain." Is this how you want to be perceived? Try "rebel" or maybe even "maverick" if you want to promote yourself as doing something different from the norm. Try "pioneer" if you want to be the first at your school to try something no one else has—yet. If you're a pioneer, you will most likely garner followers and a new crew of educators with whom you can try new things!

RULE SHARK

Let's not call attention to every mistake or infraction. Being around those types of people is exhausting. Let's focus on what is going right, then provide practice to do more of it. I actually feel we should *talk* about rule sharks (but not be rule sharks) and promote what's right and good. Let's share a rule when it needs to be shared, then guide students as to what to do next. Bonus: Let's create any classroom rules WITH students.

Educator Deanna Mascle explains how rule sharks kill writers, readers, and learners of all sorts in this blog post: **bit.ly/WSruleshark**.

49

SARCASM

The word "sarcasm" itself connotes a negative ironic expression. Irony isn't understood by many children (and some adults). I personally will wait until a student uses sarcasm with me before I know it may be okay to use it with them. If you decide to use sarcasm with autistic children or those who have autistic tendencies, please take the time to sit down and explain the meaning of the phrase you decide to use. See how #ActuallyAutistic parent Ryan Boren explains his viewpoint on sarcasm by reading his blog post on the topic: **bit.ly/WSsarcasm**.

If we're not careful, the use of sarcasm in our classrooms can be interpreted as, or even become, a form of bullying. Sarcasm includes a lot of irony and often mocks those at which it's aimed. Educator and author Dave Stuart Jr. wrote that sarcasm may have unintended negative consequences, one of them being the loss of trust in us as teachers. Even just looking at the etymology of the word shows that it can be harmful. See more of Dave's ideas here: **bit.ly/WSsarcasm2**. If you use sarcasm, please use it sparingly and know your audience.

SKYPE

Thank you, Skype creators, for being one of the first to help us confer through video! We can now simply say meet "via video" or "conference call." The same goes for Google Hangouts (currently called Meet) and Zoom, as there are now *many* ways of conferring using technology. This one is simply a pet peeve of mine; let's be specific—or generic—as the case may be. Yes, I'm one of those teachers who ask students to bring boxes of tissues at the start of the school year, not the brand name Kleenex (as my nose actually prefers Puffs).

SIMPLE/EASY

You may think a task is simple. It may not be simple for some of our peers or students. Stating that a task is "simple" prior to assigning it may turn off some students right away if they feel it is challenging for them. And what if they fail at something we introduced as simple? Consider informing them that if it seems simple for them, they may enrich their experience by moving on to more difficult tasks, adding to the task, putting their own flair on the task, etc. Also consider informing them that if this task is difficult, they may reach out for help by asking a peer, looking it up online, etc. Provide the scaffolds for tasks to help students who struggle with assignments that seem anything but easy or simple. Then we can use the word when we're teaching our students how to make difficult tasks simpler.

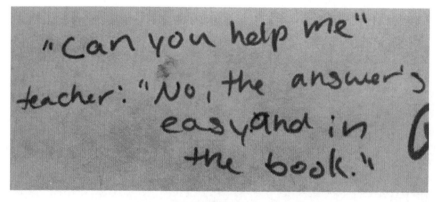

"CAN YOU HELP ME?"
TEACHER: "NO, THE ANSWER'S EASY AND IN THE BOOK."

SMART (AS A LABEL)

There are so many kinds of smart. Book smart is what many of my students think of when they hear the word "smart." What about mechanically smart? Socially smart? Street smart? Plenty of my students, whom some would call "book smart," aren't all that socially smart. If we use the word "smart," let's use it *all the time* when recognizing the various talents and skills our students display.

STEAL

Let's not "steal" other teachers' ideas. I've had some of my work shared through social media as if it were someone else's. I know I most likely did the same before I realized what I was doing. Not only is it rude, but we could be sued for it. Instead, let's collaborate with more educators so we can *use, remix, alter* or *improve upon* ideas, always giving credit where credit is due. Then it's not stealing, because no thievery has occurred. We can now use the idea with our students and let them know that we tweaked another teacher's idea. Want to go a step further with students? Let them help you create a "thank you" message for the person who shared the original idea. If we remix or improve on someone else's work while giving credit and drawing attention to their work, it is rewarding to the original creator, it helps others notice the original creator, and sharing the work more widely might even be the intent of the person who created the work in the first place.

51

Administrator and author George Couros makes additional compelling points in his post "Moving from 'Stealing' to 'Remixing' With Credit" (**bit.ly/WSsteal**).

STUCK IN THE SYSTEM

We're not stuck. We can choose to leave. Feeling stuck is an attitude. If you believe you are stuck in the educational system, it's time to be resourceful. Check with your administration to see what is mandated and what can be changed. Do the research. Have the conversations. Keep the questions coming until you can find a solution that works for you and your students. Then you can be working within the system.

STUPID (AS A LABEL)

My mom used to charge me a quarter every time I said this word. (Same for "brang" instead of "brought," which I really had trouble with, and "shut up," which cost me a dollar—and added up quickly when I was with my sister!) Sometimes the word comes out of my mouth when I feel that I personally have done something stupid. After I started collecting words for this dictionary, I heard myself say it again under my breath. Instead of calling myself "stupid," I can now change it to something more fitting, such as "forgetful," "clumsy," "not thinking it through."

If a student is planning on standing on a table, and I hear another say, "That's a stupid idea!" I like to follow up with, "It's a dangerous decision that could have serious consequences." Around educators, I've heard that certain children act stupid, certain rules or ideas are stupid, certain professional development sessions look stupid. If we think something is stupid, it might be best to keep our opinions to ourselves, change the language to express what we really mean, or simply remain quiet so as not to spread negativity. (We could also risk looking stupid ourselves when something turns out to be just the opposite.)

TASKED WITH PERFORMING A RANDOM ACT OF KINDNESS

"Our class was tasked with performing a random act of kindness for the fire department." How is it random if we're making it a task? I love the idea of random acts of kindness. Let's not push them on children; let's model performing them instead. Let's invite them to join us. Let's start with asking one student to help us execute an act of kindness each day. If you're looking for some ideas, get on your favorite social media (or simply do an internet search) and type in #raok, #payitforward, or #randomactsofkindness, or read educator Tamara Letter's book *A Passion for Kindness* (which also has a hashtag, #PassionforKindness).

TEACHERS _____

There are myriad examples of what "teachers are doing" in the media. It irks me when I see—in materials for teachers, no less—that teachers are "doing the same things they've always done, just with more expensive tools," or "not responsive to students' needs," or any number of things teachers are supposedly doing (or not doing). Teachers come from all walks of life, work in all kinds of situations, and what they do in school on any given day depends on the situation and their experiences.

Instead of making a blanket statement about teachers in general, I suggest we (the media, parents, politicians, and educators as well) go into classrooms and see what teachers are actually doing (or not doing). Imagine if visitors could schedule time to talk with those teachers and learn more about what they do and the reasons why. I'd bet that those teachers might even ask for feedback for their lessons or ideas for how to improve an activity.

Whether it's through inviting people in or sharing our work at conferences and online, let's be intentional about showing the world what we're doing. In doing so, we might just abolish those blanket statements about teachers.

TEACHERS SHOULD

"Teachers should" is another blanket statement that makes my skin crawl. Who is to say what teachers should and should not be doing in any given classroom? Administration? Parents? The media? Whoever it is, I hope they fully understand the particular situation they're governing.

Even if a slew of teachers is already doing whatever it is "they" say teachers should be doing, and even if the "should" is a good practice for some, it won't work for *all* teachers or *all* students. "Should" statements discredit those teachers who actually are doing those things and discounts those who have tried the particular tasks and moved on for something that works more effectively with their students.

In my opinion, "teachers should" statements give education a bad reputation, and we've already got enough of that going around. Once I noticed how often education articles and books use this phrase, I became aware of how many times I had used it in social media. With that awareness, I decided to use "I believe" statements instead. For example, "I believe if teachers provide opportunities for student voices to be heard, they can use it for feedback and to move forward." These

"I believe" statements could be interpreted as if teachers are already doing these things, and more are getting on board. When we see articles or blog posts that have "teachers should" followed by something we don't believe, leave a comment! Explain your own reasons why you disagree. Keep the conversation going—without the "should"s.

THE BELL DOESN'T DISMISS YOU; I DISMISS YOU.

This comes straight from my nephew's mouth. As a seventh grader, he's trying to get to classes on time, and wonders, "If the bell doesn't dismiss us, how are we supposed to know when the next class starts? I don't want to get a tardy either."

There are a multitude of reasons why we may not finish our lessons in the allotted time. Even if we don't agree that a schedule dictated by bells is the best system, we work within those confines if it's how our school day flows. The more we work in this system, the better we become. Even so, there will still be some classes when we can't get it all done. Oh well. Our students count on us to know how long the class is and plan accordingly. How about, if our lesson runs long, we try something along the lines of "We'll finish this tomorrow," "Can you please wait for one more thing?" or "Let's let Susie finish what she was saying."

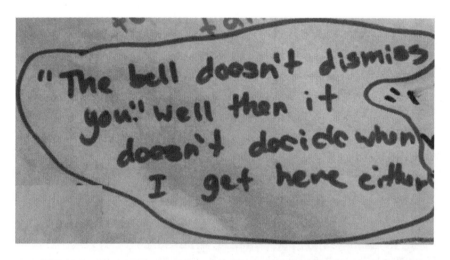

"THE BELL DOESN'T DISMISS YOU." WELL THEN IT DOESN'T DECIDE WHEN I GET HERE EITHER.

THEY WON'T SAY "YES."

There are many things we'd like to try in our classrooms, in the school, and in the district. Instead of imagining the myriad things "they" will say to shoot down our ideas, let's consider empowering ourselves. Consider "what if" in place of "they won't say yes." What if our administrators actually *did* say yes? What if they allowed us to try it with a small group? What if they said they'd consider it then set a new time to chat about it?

If you've done the research and you feel it's a valid option, empower yourself to talk to "them" to explain. The worst they could say is no, but *what if?*

THIS GROUP

"This group of kids" moves up to the next grade—every year—with a reputation they can't shake. I think this is unfair. It is not fair to label the entire group when we know darn well it's not the entire group. Worse yet, the students in that grade or class are bound to hear the rumors or feel our vibes and begin to conform to the stigma that has been attached to the group. Instead of labeling and lumping students into groups, let's offer every child, class, and grade level a "blank slate" at the start of every year and even every day.

See also: any other words used as labels

THREATS

I've had students thank me for not telling them I was going to "chop off their knee caps" or "light them on fire." (My jaw dropped when I heard that those threats were being spewed!) I've also had students thank me for not yelling at them.

Threats may seem funny to certain educators—and certain students—at the time. Some students, however, take them to heart. Their brains might not yet be wired to understand sarcasm or teasing. I hope people who chose the education profession do not actually want to inflict pain, injury, or damage to children. Let's keep school a safe space and keep the threats away. This includes threats of lowering students' grades. If students do not put their name on the upper right-hand corner of the paper, or if they turn in work a day late, let's not threaten them with a lower grade. Let's communicate with them like the professionals we are.

See also: "penalty"

THREE-MONTH VACATION

I wonder if any educators actually utter these words. Many teachers, while on summer "break," work in their garden, take graduate classes, enjoy a trip with their family, all the while wondering, "What if I did ___ next school year?" So many ideas swirl around in our minds during the summer, and we wonder how we can improve our lessons and our classroom culture.

When we are approached by other professionals and asked how we like our "three-month vacation," we could reply with, "Do you want to switch roles for the month of September? Or May? Or December? Or January?" Or we could count up the hours spent after school and on the weekends and tell them that we've already worked enough hours prior to this "break." I'm tired of this comment that perpetuates negative talk about our chosen profession. Frankly, it makes the hackles on my neck rise. They, too, could have chosen this route we took. Let's ask them why they didn't.

TOMORROW

Why wait? Try today. I use "tomorrow" when I have to check something out that students suggest, such as song lyrics, to see if they're appropriate. And then I make sure I follow through. If you've got the time in class, however, why not try today?

TOO

The word "too" has a negative connotation (when it's not being used as "also"). We can feel "too fat" or notice a person that seems "too lazy." What about "too smart for his own good," "too beautiful to be only in seventh grade," or "too happy for a Monday morning." The word "too" can make virtually any word seem like it's not a good thing.

Consider what you mean when using this word. Is what it means truly your intent? Could it be understood differently to the person hearing it? Check out this video for more thoughts on this word: **bit.ly/WStoo.**

TRAIN (VERB)

Training is fine for pets that will never leave our homes, but our learners are not pets. We should not be "training" them. Let's help young people learn instead. Let's "educate," "teach," and even "learn with" our students.

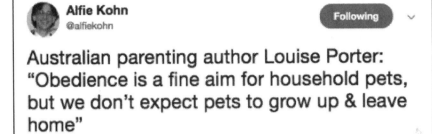

Alfie Kohn
@alfiekohn
Following ⌄

Australian parenting author Louise Porter: "Obedience is a fine aim for household pets, but we don't expect pets to grow up & leave home"

10:42 AM - 12 Nov 2018

TRICK THEM

I've heard this phrase when talking about quizzes and tests. If you are providing an assessment for students wherein they can "cheat," you may be tempted to change the order of the answers to "trick them" when they decide to cheat. There are two problems here. The first is that you're expecting students to look at other students' work. Yes, this may happen. Yes, you should probably be prepared if this does happen. But gosh darn it, they are children. They have so many stresses in their lives, and your assessment should not be one of them. If they have been given multiple opportunities in your class to work on practice problems, to revise them, to reflect on what they know and still need to know, a quiz or a test should not be one added stressor.

Secondly, take a look at the quiz or test itself. What types of questions are you asking? Gone are the days of memorization. We've got phones that act like computers for that sort of thing. Now is the time to focus on critical thinking, such as application and creativity, when it comes to our subject matter.

See also: "cheat"

TRY HARDER

Effort is something we often misjudge. How can we honestly know how much effort a person is putting into a task? When we say "try harder" to a student, it implies they are not trying as much as they are able. But what if they are? The unintended message of try harder will sound more like "you can't do this" or "you're not smart enough." Instead of putting the emphasis on effort, consider asking the student questions, or suggesting a different avenue for them to try. Try teaching. It's what we do.

TURN IT IN

We need to make learning relevant, and that includes giving our students relevant opportunities to share their work. When I work hard on something, I want others to notice it, not only my teacher. I want to share it with those I love, and sometimes I want to share it with the world.

Rather than telling students to "turn in" their work, see if you can say "publish it" instead! How can we adjust our lessons so students are doing work that matters to an authentic audience? This obviously has applications for a language arts class. Consider how it can be done in math, science, world language, history, or art.

Once we have the mindset that student work could—or *will*—be published, our lessons and activities become more relevant. Students work harder to impress an audience they have not met. We have so many safe resources for students to use to publish their work to a broader audience. Let's explore these options and tell our students they can "publish it"!

UNDERLING (AS A LABEL)

If you're on a power trip, then "underling" might find its way into your vocabulary. Before you use it, please consider the synonyms for this word, which include the following: subordinate, inferior, lackey, flunky, servant, and many more. Consider, at the very least, calling them "students," or head to the list under "Positive Vibes" at the end of this dictionary to help you find a more accurate word to represent who we instruct every day.

See also: "minion"

VAGUE ANSWERS

When I provide a vague answer, it usually means one of two things: 1) I'm not ready (or willing) to talk to you right now or 2) I have no clue. Instead of providing a vague answer, let's tell the truth. If we don't know something, let's own up to it, then proceed to learn more about it. If we are not ready to talk, let's ask the other person to postpone that question until another time, or let others speak up first.

Then there are those days when something is making us feel like crud. When a colleague asks, "How are you today?" we could answer vaguely with, "Fine," and move on with our day. I'm proposing we take a moment to share what's wrong instead. For instance, when I have a headache, it has an impact on all I do, even though I try my best not to let it affect me. If I'm asking a colleague about something, knowing they have a headache, their parent is sick, they were up all night, or they were in a fender bender on their way to work, that knowledge could make a difference in where the conversation goes from there. We could take a moment to listen, we could put off the conversation, or we could continue, knowing we could revisit another time as well. It's okay to share. We're human. Communicating clearly helps us understand one another better.

See also: "fine"

WEAKNESS

We all have areas in which we aren't strong, but the word "weakness" implies a sense of permanence. Even when we struggle to overcome weaknesses, we cannot be skilled at *everything*. Instead of pointing out where students have weaknesses—or where we ourselves have weaknesses—let's try using the word "struggles." Struggles are less personal. Struggles can be due to obstacles that we may be able to overcome. These obstacles can seem smaller when we notice them and decide to do something about them. Struggles are something that we can tackle *together*.

WE'VE ALWAYS DONE IT THIS WAY.

And the conversation ends there. What's next? The conversation needs to continue! Status quo isn't necessarily the way to go. When someone tells you, "We've always done it this way," it's time to ask loads of questions: Why have we always done it this way? What was the original reason for doing it this way? What is it accomplishing now? Can we eliminate it? If not, how can we make it better? How can we tweak it so it works better for all of us? If these questions don't keep the conversation going, it's time to ask them about the community affected by what "we've always done." Put out a survey, analyze the responses, reflect on them, and share the findings with the community. If we can keep the conversation going, we have hope that progress is on the horizon.

WHEN IS LUNCH?

Unless you're making plans to go out or check with the babysitter, try enjoying the present. Try soaking up what's happening around you. If you are in a professional development session that may not be the most exciting, see what you can get out of it. If you don't want it to be a "waste of time," realize you have some control over it. Ask questions, get into a conversation, or even challenge the presenter (respectfully) with a question or issue that is relevant to you and others in the room. Educators like to say there is no bad question, so ask questions! You never know who else in the room is wondering the same thing. You could end up taking the presenter off course—to something that may be even more valuable to you and your peers.

WHY

There are times when educators need to be asking why, especially when it comes to students' behaviors. "Why" is a great starting point. I don't want to discourage the "why"s in the world. I simply believe there's a next step.

Let's quickly move from "why" to "how." Consider this: Joy is acting out at school, tripping peers in the hallway. The first question that might pop into our discussions is "Why is she doing that?" If we cannot find the reason (Joy's not speaking to us, the victims don't have a clue, we get no information from home), then we need to quickly move on to the *how* questions: "How can we direct Joy's aggression elsewhere?" or "How can we find someone Joy will confide in?"

Education is full of "why"s—Why are we still testing students so much? Why do so many educators have two jobs? Many times, "why" questions cannot be answered easily, so in order to be more positive and productive, we can choose to focus on the "how." How can we decrease the amount of testing? How can we help students not stress about the required tests? How can we work smarter, not harder?

Next step? Ask "what." Often the "what" questions become more personal and become tasks for which we're more in control. "What can I do to alleviate stress on our students during testing?" "What can I do to help me manage my own finances?" Yes, start with "why." Then move further with more questions that can help us get closer to a solution.

WORK (AS A NOUN)

Consider where you go each day. Do you go to work? Do you go to school? Do you go to learn? When I talk to students, I make sure I use the word "school" when I talk about my profession. I don't want them to think this is "just a job" for me. I want them to know I'm at school for the long haul. I enjoy saying to students, "I've been in seventh grade for __ years! I hope you want to be here that long too!" I've also tried to take this word out of my vocabulary for when it's time to "get to work." I've tried variations, such as, "Let's get to learning" or "Let's put some effort and focus into this next task."

WORKSHEET

Worksheets are often tools teachers use to control or even simply quiet students. Other times, they are for practice of a specific skill. When possible, let's provide opportunities for making learning visible, not simply something to turn in. Who puts worksheets up in the hallways for visitors to admire? Who shares worksheets online with a class overseas? Who wants to have a video conference about a worksheet? If there's a packet of worksheets, who keeps these packets after the assessment? How are they of value to students besides passing the test? How can we change the work being done in class to be more reflective of relevant problems for students?

WRANGLER (AS A LABEL)

Our students are not horses or livestock, and we hopefully are not engaged in lengthy quarrels or disputes. Instead of "wrangling" those kindergarteners who may move like a litter of kittens when lining up for lunch, try to help them work on organizing themselves. Give the work over to the students so they can practice. Make it a routine. Adults will need to do less once children know how the task could be done more efficiently and have practiced it (many times).

XEROX

Are we still copying a ton of worksheets or packets for students? Consider trying not to use the copy machine. Consider using some sort of technology to make the work more interactive for students. When you do need to copy items, try using the word "copier" or "duplicator" instead of "Xerox," as many copy machines are now different brands. This reminds me of using the word "Kleenex" instead of "tissue." (See my pet peeve under "Skype.") A copier tip: Speak kindly to copiers when you need one. They seem to thrive better in a positive environment as well!

YELL

Not the word, per se, but the action. Children yell from the day they're born. They yell to survive when one of their basic needs is not being met. My sister and I would yell at each other growing up.

Adults don't need to yell, unless it is an issue of safety, or distance, or cheering on our favorite person or team. Although I've also had that switch tripped, causing me to lose control and yell, I've also felt so ashamed after doing so. Yelling in anger never belongs in the classroom. Stephen Marche, host of a parenting podcast, wrote a great piece for *The New York Times* that explains that yelling not only doesn't help, but it produces increased levels of anxiety, stress, and depression, while increasing behavioral problems at the same time. He also shares a specific technique to try instead, which includes naming the behavior we want and praising children when they are practicing this behavior: **bit.ly/WSyell1**. Educator Jennifer Gonzalez shares a few more reasons why it's a poor idea to yell: It's terrible role modeling, it trains students to ignore your normal voice, you may lose respect, and it creates anxiety for everyone—even the teacher across the hall. Check out more from her post here: **bit.ly/WSyell2**.

The poet Rumi may have put it best: "Raise your words, not your voice. It is rain that grows flowers, not thunder."

YOU

Try "we," or even "me" or "I." When a student acts out, instead of saying, "You're being disrespectful," we can get our message out by saying something along the lines of "I would appreciate more of your respect." As a conflict comes up with a staff member, using "we" instead of "you" creates a sense of collaboration. Imagine hearing "we can always do more" instead of "you could do more." We are in this profession dealing with stressors together. As humans, we can only control so much. When we're upset with what someone else is doing, and we cannot control it, it's time to focus on what we can control. I love Charles Swindoll's quote from *Strengthening Your Grip*: "I'm convinced that life is 10 percent what happens to me and 90 percent how I react to it."

Put the focus on what "we" can do or what "I" myself can do.

Sometimes, however, it is only right to exalt others. Use "you" in those situations! Let others know what they're doing that makes you happy or proud or has affected you positively in some way. Let them know you noticed and that they are appreciated. "You matter" is one of the most powerful phrases to use with students and with peers. When you do, tell them *why* they matter. They'll remember this powerful and positive use of the word "you."

ZIP IT/SHUT UP

My mom used to charge my sister and me a dollar each time we said, "Shut up." It's now a pet peeve of my own in class. And yet, I've heard myself say, "Zip it," which sounds much nicer, yet seems to me to have the same meaning. When asking students to be quiet, consider being *proactive* instead of *reactive*, and use these options instead:
- To show respect, let's stay quiet.
- Let's all listen so we can hear the information we'll need.

- Let's be respectful to ____ as they speak.
- Please use your ears instead of your mouth.
- Thank you for being respectful by being a great audience.

ZOO

I can only imagine what it would be like to take a class to the zoo! Some people, however, use the word "zoo" to describe classroom learning spaces. It could be when we pass a room: "That room is a zoo!" It could be the day we had: "My classroom was a zoo today!" Imagine if a child heard you. I wonder, would he think of himself as an animal? Would he decide to act a bit wild after hearing this? Would he feel trapped in your classroom, as if in a cage of sorts?

In a Tweet from a teacher who calls her school a prison, she posted the view from a school window with criss-crossed wires in them for more security. The more we say it's a prison or zoo, the more our students will believe it and want to escape it. Instead, try these alternatives: "That room had a lot of energy!" or "I'll bet those kids are learning a ton!" When it comes to windows with bars, try "We're safer behind these windows."

POSITIVE VIBES

positive—adj. 1. Characterized by or displaying certainty, acceptance, or affirmation. **2.** Measured or moving forward or in a direction of increase or progress.

[*The American Heritage Dictionary*, fourth edition, Houghton Mifflin Harcourt (2009)]

The words we choose can make a (positive or negative) difference in our lives and the lives of those around us. At the start of this book, I mentioned how we could wrongly label students. Throughout this book, I've sprinkled in labels we've used and an alternative or two to try. I think it's time I listed the positive labels I'm working to provide my students. Under these labels are adjectives we can use to describe our students. Please add your own in the margins and share them with me and with the world!

After these labels and descriptions is a list of topics I believe are worth discussing with students. These topics can be year-long discussions, depending on the age you teach and the maturity level of your students. Be sure to keep parents up to date with what you're discussing and trying in class, so they can continue the conversations at home.

LABELS THAT BUILD UP STUDENTS AND PEERS

Adventurer
Amplifier
Artist
Author
Catalyst
Change Agent
Coach
Collaborator
Comedian (If
this one comes
off as negative,
try "humorist" or
even make one up,
such as "Laugh
Generator.")
Communicator
Contributor
Creator
Decision-maker
Designer
Detective

Difference-maker
Director
Educator
Encourager
Explorer
Friend
Game-changer
Go-getter
Guide
Helper
Hero
Historian
Humorist
Informer
Innovator
Inventor
Leader
Learner
Listener
Maker
Mathematician

Mentor
Musician
Partner
Philanthropist
Pioneer
Problem-solver
Publicist
Reader
Reporter
Researcher
Risk-taker
Role Model
Scientist
Singer
Supporter
Teacher
Team Player
Teammate
Transformer
Visionary
Writer

ADJECTIVES THAT BEST DESCRIBE STUDENTS AND PEERS

Active
Collaborative
Committed (To
students and
learning!)
Courageous
Creative

Curious
Effective
Engaging
Impactful
Important
Innovative
Instrumental

Observant
Passionate
Reflective
Respectful
Thoughtful
Vivacious

TOPICS WORTH DISCUSSING THROUGHOUT THE SCHOOL YEAR

Appreciation
Balance
Bias
Choices
Collaboration
Community
Courage
Culture
Curiosity
Decision-making
Differences
Empathy
Empowerment
Failure

Feedback
Gratitude
Honesty
Hope
Humor
Kindness
Identity
Improving
Inquiry
Leadership
Learning
Listening
Mental Health
Mindfulness

Opportunities
Perspective
Practice
Privilege
Process (over Product)
Purpose
Reflection
Relationships
Respect
Strengths
Support
Teamwork
Trust

PHRASES TO USE

Time to move on to more than one word. Some positive remarks cannot be said in one simple word. Stringing the right words together can have magical effects on our relationships with peers and students. Listed here are the *magic words* you can use to produce a healthy culture at your school. After these phrases are sentence stems to try with students and peers.

PHRASES TO USE WITH CHILDREN AND ADULTS

- I appreciate you.
- I believe in you. (You have to mean this one; they'll know if you don't.)
- I don't know; let's find out.
- I hear you.
- I trust you.
- I'd love your contributions.

- I'm here for you.
- I'm listening.
- I want to learn from you.
- Let's chat again. (Then set a day and time.)
- Let's keep this conversation going.
- Let's look at a different perspective.
- Let's reflect on what went well and what we can change.
- Let's try together.
- Not yet.
- Please ____.
- Please explain further.
- Please share.
- Please share your feedback.
- Please share your ideas/thoughts.
- Show me.
- Take the lead.
- Thank you.
- We can do this.
- We should try this.
- You *matter!*
- Your feedback helped me reflect and grow.

SENTENCE STEMS TO EXPERIMENT WITH

- I was impressed by . . .
- It made my day when . . .
- Let's reflect on . . .
- Let's try . . .
- Today we get to . . .
- We're so fortunate today to . . .
- What I like about it is . . .
- Yes, and . . .

QUESTIONS

"There is no such thing as a stupid question." I've heard this phrase being poked fun at due to some of the questions we get in our classrooms. Here's the thing. If a student simply was not listening, I'm glad that child asked that "stupid" question. It's likely other students may not have been listening either. I believe questions generate discussion. Discussions can then lead to even more questions. Having lots of questions is good for reflective professionals. Sometimes, after a particularly good discussion, I walk away with more questions than when I started. I know then that I have listened and am on my way to learning even more.

There's been a huge push in education (for good reason, I believe) for classroom discussions and assessments to be more about the meaning of the lesson, instead of rote memory. Educators have been encouraged to not ask questions that only prove who read the text or who can regurgitate facts, but questions that are more open-ended or, better yet, questions asked by the students themselves. I'd think that our questions in our professional spheres would be along those lines, too—questions that are open-ended and make us think about the future and what is right and good for our students. With that in mind, I've been collecting all sorts of questions. These questions are for our own children, our students, our colleagues, and ourselves. I believe that the right question can propel our thinking and our planning.

The right question will stir the passion inside us to help us move—to help us shift toward a better direction. No matter how skilled a teacher we may think we are, there is always room to grow. Questions can help us grow and flourish. We need to continue to ask more questions. Asking questions will help keep the conversations going about what is right and good for our students (and ourselves), and it will help us to continually reflect.

Once you decide your own students need to be asking more and better questions, check out the Right Question Institute *(rightquestion.org)* and their QFT—the Question Formulation Technique.

The following are just a small sample of questions for various situations or audiences. They can be used at the start or end of a lesson, in a quick conversation, or as guides for larger conversations or conversations that will continue the course of your school year. I would love to hear the questions you ask that help you move forward in your own education. Please write them in the margins, share them with me, and I'll add them to my own tool kit to keep the conversations going!

QUESTIONS TO ASK CHILDREN

- How are you doing/feeling?
- How is your energy level?
- How can I improve . . .?
- How can we . . .?
- How can we lower/raise our level of energy today?
- How can we make this more relevant to us?
- How can we share our ideas today?
- How can you change the world a bit today?
- How can you lead us today?
- How will we be kind today?
- How will we work toward our goal?
- How would you do this differently?
- How would you do this differently next time?
- Now what?
- What are our next steps?
- What are your strengths?
- What did we learn?
- What do you notice?
- What do you think?
- What do you want to learn?
- What does your heart say?
- What does your mind say?
- What drives you?
- What else?
- What is on your mind?
- What is our call to action?
- What is the real challenge?
- What is your choice?
- What is your genius?
- What makes you excited to come to school?
- What makes you think that?
- What makes you unique?
- What other perspectives can we consider?
- What questions do you have? (Math teacher André Sasser explains how this question has replaced "Who has a question?" in her class and why: **bit.ly/WSquestions1**.)

- What technology can help us with this task?
- What would you do if you were me? (Administrator and author George Couros explains how this question can equip students to find their own way. I'd add that if asked of peers, it shows vulnerability and that it's okay—and beneficial—to ask for help. Check out his post here: **bit.ly/WSquestions2**.)
- What would you like to tell me?
- When can we meet about this again?
- Which would you rather . . . ?
- Who can provide us with some assistance?
- Who can we connect with in order to learn . . . ?
- Who do you want to learn alongside?
- Who feels they can teach us something today?
- Who needs a high five (a smile, a quiet space to learn, etc.)?
- Who needs some assistance?
- Who wants to take on this challenge?
- Who would like to share?
- Why do you think that?
- Why should we . . . ?

QUESTIONS TO ASK COLLEAGUES

- Can we join forces (combine our talents) in order to . . . ?
- Could the students be doing this? (Administrator and author George Couros explains how this question posed to colleagues could lead to student empowerment in his post here: **bit.ly/WSquestions3**.)
- How are you?
- How can I help?
- How can I improve . . . ?
- How can I make this better?
- How can we . . . ?
- How can we help students . . . ?
- How can we make this more relevant to us?
- How can we move past this?
- How have other schools accomplished this?
- How have other schools approached this?
- What are our next steps?
- What are our priorities?

- What are we missing?
- What are your strengths?
- What are your thoughts?
- What can I do for you?
- What can make this better?
- What can we do next?
- What did we learn?
- What do you think?
- What do you want to accomplish?
- What does your heart say?
- What does your mind say?
- What drives you?
- What else?
- What has been useful in the past?
- What if we . . .?
- What is in our blind spot?
- What is on your mind?
- What is the best tool for this?
- What is the challenge?
- What is your goal?
- What is your passion?
- What makes you excited to come to school?
- What makes you think that?
- What more would you like to add?
- What technology can help us with this task?
- What would you do if you were me?
- What's our priority?
- What's stopping you?
- When can we schedule time to discuss this further?
- Where can we learn more?
- Where should we put our energy or focus?
- Which idea should we try first?
- Which would you rather . . .?
- Who can we go to for help?
- Who is skilled at this?
- Who wants to take on this challenge?
- Why?
- Why do you believe this is best for children?

- Why not?
- Why should we . . .?
- Why shouldn't we . . .?
- Will you please help me with . . .?
- Would you be willing . . .? (If we're looking to persuade, Elizabeth Stokoe, professor of social interaction at Loughborough University, says to try using the word "willing" instead of "would you be able," "would you like to," or "would you be interested." See more in a post from *The Guardian* here: **bit.ly/WSquestions4**.)

POINTS ABOUT
POSITIVE POSSIBILITIES

possibility—**n.** *1.* The fact or state of being possible, *2.* Something that is possible. *3.* **Possibilities.** Potentiality for favorable or interesting results.

[*The American Heritage Dictionary*, fourth edition, Houghton Mifflin Harcourt (2009)]

People say I'm an optimist. I'm not sure if it's true. I do not "usually expect a favorable outcome," as my *American Heritage Dictionary* says of optimists. I will admit that I'd rather look for the good than the bad in any situation. My outlook is not just a product of the name my parents gave me (although that does help). I'm an optimist because I am constantly grateful for all I have—the people who surround me, the roof over my head, the clothes on my back, the food on the table. When I was struggling in my first marriage, one way I got through it was when I awoke each day, I recognized it as a new day. Fresh. A clean slate. The possibilities were (are) endless. Mornings were (are) full of hope. This became my survival gear, and it got me far.

I've learned to bring this positivity into the classroom. Each day with each class, I start fresh, asking students how their morning or day is going. I'll ask them something about the day prior, or I'll ask them to share a celebration. I say, "Hello!" and "How are you?" no matter what happened with the curriculum or their behavior the day before. In the hallway, instead of asking, "Where's that signed permission slip?" (that's three days late), I start fresh and ask instead, "How are you today?" The first question sounds like it's full of blame, and the second sounds like I care—and I do! If students think I don't care about them, why should they care about me or our class?

I frequently hear teachers talk about the stressors that are common in education. They often start with phrases such as "my administration now expects *this*," "the parents want me to do *this*," "the students aren't doing *this*." Simply hearing about these can elevate stress levels with our colleagues and with our students. Many of these stressors are not something we can change. What we *can* change, however, is our focus.

Instead of talking about what makes us stressed, we could talk about what helps us relieve stress. Simply talking about stress-relieving strategies can put us in a calmer state of mind, with smiles on our faces. Add a lame joke and some laughter, and we suddenly are releasing helpful endorphins into our bodies.

One of the stressors that we can shift from negative to positive is feedback. When we ask for feedback from peers, parents, or students, we're asking so we can improve. When we receive this feedback, it can hurt. No matter how much positive feedback we receive, it's our human tendency to focus on the negative. Asking for feedback is a risk we take in order to grow. Sure, we want to hear positive feedback, but when we receive corrective or contrary feedback, we can grow! Here's just one example: Every time a parent opposes ideas I have in the classroom, I learn how to better communicate with parents the next year. I've gone back and reassessed what I'm doing: Is it right for my students (aka their children)? I've created short video explanations if I feel they aren't reading the notes home. I've improved the communication between us.

Feedback can hurt—literally. It has caused me a migraine or two, and it has brought me to tears. When we ask for feedback, we need to be ready to grow from it. To learn from it. And then to act on it. This is especially true for daily feedback from students. When they share their thoughts and ideas, what happens if we don't act on it? They'll figure it out. They'll then learn to not share their ideas anymore. Why should they, if we aren't responding to them? View students' words, their facial expressions, and their work (or lack thereof) as feedback.

If we take the positive route of asking for and responding to feedback, our class culture will grow and bloom.

Other stressors come unbidden. Some days begin with someone cutting us off in traffic, and of course they end up braking right in front of us at the very next red light. When we get to school, we pass that one teacher who never responds to our "good morning." The refrigerator door was accidentally left open all night so our yogurt may be spoiled; oh, and someone took our water bottle—again. ("It's THEFT!" our brain shouts.) What about those days? How will our students suffer because of the events in our morning? When a student complains (again) that they're tired, and you yourself spent much of last night taking care of a sick child or pet at home, or a sick parent at the hospital, or even yourself, what's your response?

On those days, we have to be in charge of our attitude. Although it's not always possible to do, I make an extra effort to start anew with each teacher and student. I put on that smile, release those endorphins, and wonder, *What is this person in front of me going through? How can I be the positive person in their day?* No, it doesn't always work. Sometimes I feel too exhausted. Sometimes I just don't have the energy. Sometimes I want to wallow in my own self-pity. Most of the time, however, when I put forth the effort, it makes my own day brighter.

Starting with a clean slate, asking peers and students, "How are you today?" can help me understand what they're going through. It can take the focus off my own issues. It can put my heart in the right place, and many times, makes me more grateful for all I do have in this life. Asking about others, helping when we are able (even if it's just to lend an ear), can improve our own mental health and help us build relationships with those around us.

This profession we've chosen is not easy. I imagine being a child in the school system today isn't too easy either. The more positive our word choice, our attitudes, and our actions, the more possibilities will open up for us to have a greater impact on one another and on those young learners we serve.

How will you find your voice and use it when you hear negative language in schools? How will you elevate and amplify your voice so it reaches more students and colleagues?

JOY KIRR

This book is one route I'm taking to promote positivity. Our students will remember what we said—the good and the bad. Let's choose our words to make a positive difference in people's lives. To share your own word shift ideas with me and with the world, use the hashtag #WordShift on your favorite social media platform, so we can nullify negativity and promote positivity. Thank you for joining me in this endeavor!

BIBLIOGRAPHY

Tweet #CUE18 March 16, 2018
   https://twitter.com/thomascmurray/status/974742852600152064

Swindoll, Charles. *Strengthening Your Grip: How to Be Grounded in a Chaotic World.* Nashville: Worthy Publishing, 2015, revised edition.

ACKNOWLEDGMENTS

acknowledge—**1a.** To admit the existence, reality, or truth of. **b.** To recognize as being valid or having force or power. **2a.** To express recognition of. **b.** To express thanks or gratitude for.

[*The American Heritage Dictionary*, fourth edition, Houghton Mifflin Harcourt (2009)]

THANK YOU to my family, who started me with language acquisition. My parents and then sister spoke bits and pieces of French, German, and Spanish, to keep me in the dark about presents or things I wasn't supposed to know. Once I took four years of French, two years of Spanish, one year of German, and a week of Russian (at the library, no less), I added sign language to my repertoire, all thanks to your encouragement. (I can't believe I never tried to learn the shorthand you used!)

THANK YOU to the myriad educators and administrators I've worked with over the years. Listening to your vocabulary, both strong and subtle, has helped me shape my messages with students and school personnel and let me try new avenues in my own teaching.

THANK YOU to the many students through these exciting years whom I've served as one of your teachers. You teach me so many new words, phrases, games, and even dance moves. I'm trying to go at this teaching thing "full send." (I used to say "all in," and can now see how "full send" can be even more powerful!)

THANK YOU to my husband, who always, through role modeling, encourages me to choose the word I truly mean. From the start of all of our letters back and forth, you've helped make choosing the most accurate word a priority in my life. I look forward to every discussion we have, as you listen with patience, respond with thoughtfulness, and never dispense any judgment—only a seeking to understand, coupled with tender love and care.

THANK YOU to the entire crew of DBC Inc. Your encouragement, guidance, and support has helped me spread my message(s) far and wide. I know your work with me and other educator-authors has helped educators around the globe consider, reflect upon what we're doing in front of students and behind the scenes, and try our best for students and peers as we keep the conversations going.

MORE FROM

Since 2012, DBCI has been publishing books that inspire and equip educators to be their best. For more information on our DBCI titles or to purchase bulk orders for your school, district, or book study, visit DaveBurgessconsulting.com/DBCIbooks.

MORE FROM THE PIRATE™ SERIES

- *Teach Like a PIRATE* by Dave Burgess
- *eXPlore Like a Pirate* by Michael Matera
- *Learn Like a Pirate* by Paul Solarz
- *Play Like a Pirate* by Quinn Rollins
- *Run Like a Pirate* by Adam Welcome

LEAD LIKE A PIRATE™ SERIES

- *Lead Like a PIRATE* by Shelley Burgess and Beth Houf
- *Balance Like a Pirate* by Jessica Cabeen, Jessica Johnson, and Sarah Johnson
- *Lead beyond Your Title* by Nili Bartley
- *Lead with Culture* by Jay Billy
- *Lead with Literacy* by Mandy Ellis

LEADERSHIP & SCHOOL CULTURE

- *Culturize* by Jimmy Casas
- *Escaping the School Leader's Dunk Tank* by Rebecca Coda and Rick Jetter
- *From Teacher to Leader* by Starr Sackstein
- *The Innovator's Mindset* by George Couros
- *Kids Deserve It!* by Todd Nesloney and Adam Welcome
- *Let Them Speak* by Rebecca Coda and Rick Jetter
- *The Limitless School* by Abe Hege and Adam Dovico
- *The Pepper Effect* by Sean Gaillard
- *The Principled Principal* by Jeffrey Zoul and Anthony McConnell
- *Relentless* by Hamish Brewer
- *The Secret Solution* by Todd Whitaker, Sam Miller, and Ryan Donlan
- *Start. Right. Now.* by Todd Whitaker, Jeffrey Zoul, and Jimmy Casas
- *Stop. Right. Now.* by Jimmy Casas and Jeffrey Zoul
- *Unmapped Potential* by Julie Hasson and Missy Lennard
- *They Call Me "Mr. De"* by Frank DeAngelis
- *Your School Rocks* by Ryan McLane and Eric Lowe

TECHNOLOGY & TOOLS

- *50 Things You Can Do with Google Classroom* by Alice Keeler and Libbi Miller
- *50 Things to Go Further with Google Classroom* by Alice Keeler and Libbi Miller
- *140 Twitter Tips for Educators* by Brad Currie, Billy Krakower, and Scott Rocco
- *Block Breaker* by Brian Aspinall
- *Code Breaker* by Brian Aspinall
- *Google Apps for Littles* by Christine Pinto and Alice Keeler
- *Master the Media* by Julie Smith
- *Shake Up Learning* by Kasey Bell
- *Social LEADia* by Jennifer Casa-Todd
- *Teaching Math with Google Apps* by Alice Keeler and Diana Herrington
- *Teachingland* by Amanda Fox and Mary Ellen Weeks

TEACHING METHODS & MATERIALS

- *All 4s and 5s* by Andrew Sharos
- *The Classroom Chef* by John Stevens and Matt Vaudrey
- *Ditch That Homework* by Matt Miller and Alice Keeler
- *Ditch That Textbook* by Matt Miller
- *Don't Ditch That Tech* by Matt Miller, Nate Ridgway, and Angelia Ridgway
- *EDrenaline Rush* by John Meehan
- *Educated by Design* by Michael Cohen, The Tech Rabbi
- *The EduProtocol Field Guide* by Marlena Hebern and Jon Corippo
- *Instant Relevance* by Denis Sheeran
- *LAUNCH* by John Spencer and A.J. Juliani
- *Make Learning MAGICAL* by Tisha Richmond
- *Pure Genius* by Don Wettrick
- *The Revolution* by Darren Ellwein and Derek McCoy
- *Shift This!* by Joy Kirr
- *Spark Learning* by Ramsey Musallam
- *Sparks in the Dark* by Travis Crowder and Todd Nesloney
- *Table Talk Math* by John Stevens
- *The Wild Card* by Hope and Wade King
- *The Writing on the Classroom Wall* by Steve Wyborney

85

INSPIRATION, PROFESSIONAL GROWTH & PERSONAL DEVELOPMENT

- *Be REAL* by Tara Martin
- *Be the One for Kids* by Ryan Sheehy
- *Creatively Productive* by Lisa Johnson
- *The EduNinja Mindset* by Jennifer Burdis
- *Empower Our Girls* by Lynmara Colón and Adam Welcome
- *The Four O'Clock Faculty* by Rich Czyz
- *How Much Water Do We Have?* by Pete and Kris Nunweiler
- *P Is for Pirate* by Dave and Shelley Burgess
- *A Passion for Kindness* by Tamara Letter
- *The Path to Serendipity* by Allyson Apsey
- *Sanctuaries* by Dan Tricarico
- *Shattering the Perfect Teacher Myth* by Aaron Hogan

- *Stories from Webb* by Todd Nesloney
- *Talk to Me* by Kim Bearden
- *The Zen Teacher* by Dan Tricarico
- *Through the Lens of Serendipity* by Allyson Apsey

CHILDREN'S BOOKS
- *Beyond Us* by Arron Polansky
- *Dolphins in Trees* by Aaron Polansky
- *The Princes of Serendip* by Allyson Apsey
- *I Want to Be a Lot* by Ashley Savage
- *Zom-Be a Design Thinker* by Amanda Fox

ABOUT THE AUTHOR

JOY KIRR is sought after for her keynotes on shifting the culture of classes and for her workshops on how to bring student-directed learning into the classroom. Currently teaching seventh graders in a truly supportive district in Arlington Heights, Illinois, Joy is passionate about students owning their own learning. She enjoys being known as a "Genius Hour Evangelist" and is grateful for how her students have stepped up their learning while giving and receiving feedback in lieu of grades. Presenting around the nation has helped Joy spread the message that educators need to strive for all children to become lifelong learners.

Joy earned her bachelor's degree in special education with an emphasis on deaf and hard-of-hearing in 1995, and she later earned her master's degree in reading from Northern Illinois University. Recently, she was nominated for a Golden Apple award for excellence and teaching in Illinois. Joy has been a National Board Certified Teacher since 2007. Her first book, *Shift This: How to Implement Gradual Changes for Massive Impact in Your Classroom,* came out in May of 2017. Find out more about Joy or connect with her at **ShiftThis.weebly.com**.

Made in the USA
San Bernardino, CA
28 July 2019

Get a Vocabulary Upgrade with *WORD SHIFT*

Does it feel as if students, colleagues, or administrators are making your school year difficult? Do negative thoughts cloud your day? Maybe it's time to shift your thinking.

The language we've been exposed to and the words we use when we talk about others (and ourselves) all have an impact on the way we view the world and the people in it. More importantly, as educators, what we say shapes the way our learners think about themselves and their place in the world.

If you want less negativity and more positivity in your life, classroom, and school, start by changing the words you use each day. Make your language match what you really want to believe and what you really want to happen. With **Word Shift** by **Joy Kirr**, you'll never be at a loss for just the right positive word.

Words matter. Choose yours wisely.

"Joy Kirr's book, *Word Shift*, is an important book for all educators because it draws attention to both the potential harm and benefit of labels, especially when we apply them to students."
—**Jimmy Casas**, educator, author, speaker, leadership coach

"I highly recommend this book and can't wait to participate in the ensuing conversations that it will, no doubt, spark within our community."
—**Sarah Thomas, PhD**, founder, EduMatch

"*Word Shift* is just what every educator and parent needs on their bookshelves to pull out when wondering what and how to say something with their children."
—**Barbara Bray**, creative learning strategist, author

ISBN 978-1-949595-56-
9000

Dave Burgess Consulting, Inc.

#WordShift

9 781949 595567

A Dragon Walks into a Meeting

A Tactical Guide to Client Management

John Brown
& Fred Fuller